CAMBRIDGE LIBRARY COLLECTION

Books of enduring scholarly value

Education

This series focuses on educational theory and practice, particularly in the context of eighteenth- and nineteenth-century Europe and its colonies, and America. During this period, the questions of who should be educated, to what age, to what standard and using what curriculum, were widely debated. The reform of schools and universities, the drive towards improving women's education, and the movement for free (or at least low-cost) schools for the poor were all major concerns both for governments and for society at large. The books selected for reissue in this series discuss key issues of their time, including the 'appropriate' levels of instruction for the children of the working classes, the emergence of adult education movements, and proposals for the higher education of women. They also cover topics that still resonate today, such as the nature of education, the role of universities in the diffusion of knowledge, and the involvement of religious groups in establishing and running schools.

An Introduction to Botany

From a prosperous London Quaker family, the author Priscilla Wakefield (1751–1832) wrote educational books for children, and one work for adults, *Reflections on the Present Condition of the Female Sex* (1798), also reissued in this series. This 1796 book on botany, a science which 'contributes to health of body and cheerfulness of disposition' but is difficult to study because of its Latin nomenclature and the cost of textbooks, offers a simple introduction for children through the medium of letters between sisters, as 'Felicia' shares with 'Constance' her growing understanding of plant science. Felicia's governess is a follower of Linnaeus, whose classificatory system is described as 'the one universally adopted', and by the twenty-eighth and final letter, Felicia is describing the class *Cryptogamia*. This illustrated account in simple language gives an insight into the level of education thought appropriate for young girls at the end of the eighteenth century.

T0381632

Cambridge University Press has long been a pioneer in the reissuing of out-of-print titles from its own backlist, producing digital reprints of books that are still sought after by scholars and students but could not be reprinted economically using traditional technology. The Cambridge Library Collection extends this activity to a wider range of books which are still of importance to researchers and professionals, either for the source material they contain, or as landmarks in the history of their academic discipline.

Drawing from the world-renowned collections in the Cambridge University Library and other partner libraries, and guided by the advice of experts in each subject area, Cambridge University Press is using state-of-the-art scanning machines in its own Printing House to capture the content of each book selected for inclusion. The files are processed to give a consistently clear, crisp image, and the books finished to the high quality standard for which the Press is recognised around the world. The latest print-on-demand technology ensures that the books will remain available indefinitely, and that orders for single or multiple copies can quickly be supplied.

The Cambridge Library Collection brings back to life books of enduring scholarly value (including out-of-copyright works originally issued by other publishers) across a wide range of disciplines in the humanities and social sciences and in science and technology.

An
Introduction to Botany

In a Series of
Familiar Letters, with Illustrative Engravings

PRISCILLA WAKEFIELD

CAMBRIDGE
UNIVERSITY PRESS

University Printing House, Cambridge, CB2 8BS, United Kingdom

Cambridge University Press is part of the University of Cambridge.
It furthers the University's mission by disseminating knowledge in the pursuit of
education, learning and research at the highest international levels of excellence.

www.cambridge.org
Information on this title: www.cambridge.org/9781108077217

This edition first published 1796
This digitally printed version 2015

ISBN 978-1-108-07721-7 Paperback

AN

INTRODUCTION

TO

BOTANY,

IN

A SERIES OF

FAMILIAR LETTERS,

WITH ILLUSTRATIVE ENGRAVINGS.

———————————

BY PRISCILLA WAKEFIELD,

AUTHOR OF MENTAL IMPROVEMENT, LEISURE
HOURS, &c.

———————————

LONDON:

PRINTED FOR E. NEWBERRY, ST. PAUL'S CHURCH-
YARD; DARTON AND HARVEY, GRACECHURCH-
STREET; AND VERNOR AND HOOD,
BIRCHIN-LANE.

———

M,DCC,XCVI.

PREFACE.

THE defign of the following Introduction to Botany, is to cultivate a tafte in young perfons for the ftudy of nature, which is the moft familiar means of introducing fuitable ideas of the attributes of the Divine Being, by exemplifying them in the order and harmony of the vifible creation. Children are endowed with curiofity and activity, for the purpofe of acquiring knowledge. Let us avail ourfelves of thefe natural propenfities, and direct them to the purfuit of the moft judicious objects: none can be better adapted to inftruct, and at the fame time amufe, than the beauties of nature, by which they are continually furrounded. The ftructure of a feather or a flower is more likely to imprefs their minds with a juft notion of Infinite Power and Wifdom, than the moft profound difcourfes on fuch abftract fubjects, as are beyond
the

the limits of their capacity to comprehend. In the important bufinefs of forming the human mind, the inclination and pleafure of the pupil fhould be confulted; in order to render leffons effectual, they fhould pleafe, and be fought rather as indulgencies, than avoided as laborious toils. Botany is a branch of Natural Hiftory that poffeffes many advantages; it contributes to health of body and cheerfulnefs of difpofition, by prefenting an inducement to take air and exercife; it is adapted to the fimpleft capacity, and the objects of its inveftigation offer themfelves without expence or difficulty, which renders them attainable to every rank in life; but with all thefe allurements, till of late years, it has been confined to the circle of the learned, which may be attributed to thofe books that treated of it, being principally written in Latin; a difficulty that deterred many, particularly the female fex, from attempting to obtain the knowledge of a fcience, thus defended, as it were, from their approach. Much is due to thofe of our own countrymen, who firft introduced ed this delightful volume of nature to popular notice, by prefenting it in our native language ; their labours have been a means of rendering it very generally ftudied, and it is now confidered as a neceffary addition to an accomplifhed education. May it become a fubftitute for fome of the trifling, not to fay pernicious, objects, that too frequently occupy the leifure of young ladies of fafhionable manners, and, by employing their faculties rationally, act as an antidote to levity and idlenefs. As there are many admirable Englifh books now extant upon the fubject, it may require fome apology for obtruding the prefent work upon the public. It appeared that every thing hitherto publifhed, was too expenfive, as well as too diffufe and fcientific, for the purpofe of teaching the elementary parts to children or young perfons; it was therefore thought, that a book of a moderate price, and divefted as much as poffible of technical terms, introduced in an eafy familiar form, might be acceptable.

TABLE

TABLE OF CONTENTS.

b

LETTER

LETTER X.

LETTER XI.

LETTER XII.

LETTER XIII.

LETTER XIV.

Lily

LETTER

AN

INTRODUCTION

TO

B O T A N Y.

L E T T E R I.

FELICIA TO CONSTANCE.

DEAR SISTER,   *Shrubbery, February* 1.

As it is an unufual thing for us to be feparated, I do not doubt, but we equally feel the pain of being at a diftance from each other; when I confider, that you are really gone to pafs the whole fummer with my aunt, and that I have parted with the beloved companion of my walks and amufements, I think I fhall but half enjoy either, during the fine feafon that is approaching. With you, indeed, the cafe will be rather different; new fcenes will prefent themfelves, which will entertain by their novelty and variety, and the kind attentions of my aunt and coufins will compenfate in degree for the ab-

B   fence

fence of thofe friends you have left at home. Every place here looks folitary, efpecially our own apartment, and our favourite haunts in the garden. Even the approach of fpring, which is marked by the appearance of fnow drops and crocuffes, affords me but little pleafure; my kind mother, ever attentive to my happinefs, concurs with my governefs in checking this depreffion of fpirits, and infifts upon my having recourfe to fome interefting employment that fhall amufe me, and pafs away the time while you are abfent; my fondnefs for flowers has induced my mother to propofe Botany, as fhe thinks it will be beneficial to my health, as well as agreeable, by exciting me to ufe more air and exercife than I fhould do, without fuch a motive; becaufe books fhould not be depended upon alone, recourfe muft be had to the natural fpecimens growing in fields and gardens; how fhould I enjoy this purfuit in your company, my dear fifter! but as that is impoffible at prefent, I will adopt the neareft fubftitute I can obtain, by communicating to you the refult of every leffon. You may compare my defcriptions with the flowers themfelves, and, by thus mutually purfuing the fame objeɛt, we may reciprocally improve each other. I am impatient to make a beginning, but am full of apprehenfion of the number of hard words at the entrance. However, I am refolved not to be deterred by this difficulty ; perfeverance and patience will over come it ; and as I know the eafy method of inftruction adopted by my dear governefs in other fciences, I confide in her fkill to render this eafy and pleafant. Farewell.

FELICIA.

LETTER II.

Shrubbery, February 10.

THE morning being fine tempted us abroad. Botany fupplied us with fubjects for converfation. Mrs. Snelgrove took the opportunity of remarking, that a perfect plant confifts of the root, the trunk or ftem, the leaves, the fupports, flower, and fruit ; (for botanically fpeaking) by fruit in herbs, as well as in trees, is underftood the whole formation of the feed : and as each part needs a particular explanation to a novice, fhe began her lecture by pointing out the ufes of the root. The firft, and moft obvious, is that of enabling the plant to ftand firmly in the

B 2   ground,

ground, by ferving as a balance to the head. By what means could the enormous oaks in the park be kept upright and fixed, but by their extenfive turgid roots: they ferve as a counterpoife againft the weight of the trunk and branches. The chief nourifhment of the plant is received by the radicle, or fibrous part of the roots, that, like fo many mouths, abforb the nutricious juices from the earth. The root alfo performs the part of a parent, by preferving the embryo plants in its bofom, during the feverity of winter, in form of bulbs or buds: bulbs are properly but large buds, eyes, or gems, including the future plants. Nature is an œconomift, and is fparing of this curious provifion, againft the cold, where it is unneceffary. In warm countries, few plants are furnifhed with winter buds. Roots are diftinguifhed by different names, according to their forms; as fibrous, bulbous, and tuberous, with many other leffer diftinctions, expreffive of their manner of growth.

The next part of a plant, that claims our notice, is the trunk or ftem, which rifes out of the root, and fupports the flower, leaves, &c. The trunk of trees and fhrubs, (and it is fuppofed, that the ftem of the more diminutive kinds of plants, in the fame manner) confifts of feveral diftinct parts; as the bark, the wood, the fap-veffels, correfponding to the the blood-veffels in animals;

the

the pith, the tracheæ or air veficles, and the web
or tiffue ; each of thefe parts has its peculiar ufe,
and its conftruction is admirably adapted to its
purpofe. The bark of plants feems to perform
the fame offices to them, that the fkin does to
animals ; it clothes and defends them from injury, inhales the moifture of the air, and extracts,
or conveys from the plant the fuperfluity of
moift particles. The caufe of evergreens retaining their foliage during the winter, is fuppofed
to arife from an abundant quantity of oil in
their barks, which preferves them from the effects of cold. The bark (as well as the wood)
is fupplied with innumerable veffels, which convey the fluids to and from every part of the
plant ; the wood alfo is furnifhed with others,
which contain air, and is diftributed throughout
its fubftance. The ftability of trees and fhrubs
confifts in the wood, which correfponds with the
bones of animals. The feat of life feems to re-
fide in the pith or medullary fubftance, which is
a fine tiffue of veffels originating in the centre.
The fluids of plants are the fap, analogous to
the blood of animals ; and the proper juice,
which is of various colours and confiftence in
different individuals ; as white or milky in the
dandelion, refinous in the fir, and producing gum
in cherry or plum trees, &c. Hoping that I
have given you fuch a clear defcription of the

root

root and ftem, as will enable you to form a general idea of their parts and ufes, I fhall proceed to
leaves, which contribute, at the fame time, to the
benefit and ornament of the plant. I need not tell
you, that the variety of their forms and manner of
growth is great; your own obfervation has long
fince informed you of this particular, and pre-
pared you to underftand the terms by which botanifts arrange them, according to their forms
and fhapes; as fimple, compound, rough, fmooth,
round, oval, heart fhaped, &c. thefe minutiæ
muft be learned by referring to plates. Leaves
are fuppofed to anfwer the purpofe of lungs,
and, by their inclination to be moved by the
wind, in fome degree, ferve alfo thofe of mufcles
and mufcular motions. They are very porous
on both their furfaces, and inhale and exhale
freely. The annual fun-flower is an extraordinary inftance of this faƈt; it is faid to perfpire
nineteen times as much as a man, in twenty-four
hours. Fine weather encourages the perfpira-
tion of vegetables; but in heavy, moift, and wet
weather, the inhalation exceeds. The effluvia
of plants is thought unwholefome to perfons of
delicate conftitutions, but particularly fo at night
and in a dull ftate of the atmofphere; but it is
worth obferving, that the air emitted from the
leaves is never prejudicial; that which is noxious proceeds from the corollas only.

The

The next parts to be confidered, are the fupports or props; by thefe are meant certain external parts of plants, which are ufeful to fupport and defend them from enemies and injuries,
or for the fecretion of fome fluid, that is baneful
or difagreeable to thofe infects that would otherwife hurt them. They are divided into feven
kinds: 1ft, Tendrils; fmall fpiral ftrings, by
which fome plants, that are not ftrong enough
to ftand alone, fuftain themfelves by embracing
trees, fhrubs, or other fupports; the honeyfuckle
and birdweed afford examples of this. 2dly,
Floral leaves; are fmall leaves placed near the
flower, fmaller, and moftly of a different form
from thofe of the plant. 3dly, Scales; fmall
leafy appendages, fituated on either fide, or a
little below the leaf, to protect it, when firft
emerging from the bud. 4thly, Foot ftalks;
thefe fupport the leaf, and defend and convey
nourifhment to the infant bud. 5thly, Flower
ftalks, or foot ftalks, to the flower and fruit.
6thly, Arms; a general term for the offenfive
parts of plants, fuch as thorns, prickles, ftings,
&c. 7thly, Pubes; a name applied to the de-
fenfive parts of plants, fuch as hairs, wool, a
certain hoary whitenefs, hooks, briftles, glands,
clamminefs, and vifcidity. In order to enliven
a dry detail of names, and a mere defcription of
parts, Mrs. Snelgrove favoured me with an ac-

count

count of some curious contrivances of nature, observed in some particular plants, for their defence against insects, or larger animals, that would, without this precaution, greatly annoy them; and as I know the pleasure you take in such recitals, I shall repeat them to you, before I close this long letter. The viscous matter, which surrounds the stalks, under the flowers of the catchfly, prevents various insects from plundering the honey, or devouring the pollen, which fertilizes the seed. In the dionæa muscipula, or Venus's fly-trap, there is a still more wonderful means of preventing the depredations of insects. The leaves are armed with long teeth, like the antenna of insects, and lie spread upon the ground round the stem; they are so irritable, that when an insect creeps upon them, they fold up, and crush or pierce it to death. The flower of the arum muscivorum has the smell of carrion, which invites the flies to lay their eggs in the chamber of the flower; but the worms, which are hatched from these eggs, are unable to make their escape from their prison, being prevented by the hairs pointing inwards, which has given the name of fly-eater to this flower. The same purpose is effected in the dypsacus, vulgarly called teazel, by a bason or receptacle of water, placed round each joint of the stem.

The

The naufeous and pungent juices of fome vegetables, and the fragrance of others, are beftowed upon them in common with thorns and prickles for their defence againft the depredations of animals. Many trees and fhrubs fupply grateful food to a variety of creatures, and would be quickly devoured, were they not armed with thorns and ftings, which protect them not only againft fome kinds of infects, but alfo againft the naked mouths of quadrupeds. It is worth remarking, as a farther analogy between plants and animals, that the former frequently lofe their thorns, &c. by cultivation, as wild animals are deprived of their ferocity, by living in a domeftic ftate, under the government and protection of man. My letter is already fpun out to a tedious length, I muft, therefore, referve the defcription of the fructification till a future oppor tunity.—Adieu : your

FELICIA

LETTER III.

Shrubbery, February 18.

THE approbation you exprefs, my dear Conftance, of my endeavours to amufe you with an
account of my botanical lectures, encourages
me to proceed, though with great diffidence, as I
find the fubject becomes more intricate as I advance. The fructification includes the flower
and fruit, and contains the whole procefs of perfecting the feeds. It confifts of feven parts;
and, to illuftrate them, I have fketched fome particulars from the lily, &c.

1. The (calyx) cup, or empalement, *a.*
2. The (corolla) bloffom, petals, or flower-
   leaves, *b.*
3. The (ftamina) threads or chives, *c.*
4. The (piftillum) ftyle or pointal, *d.*
5. The (pericarpium) feed veffel, *e.*
6. The feed or fruit, *f.*
7. The (receptaculum) receptacle, or bafe, *g.*

Some flowers poffefs all thefe parts, others are
deficient in fome of them; but the chives or the
pointals, or both, are effential, and to be found
in all, either in flowers on the fame plant, or in
different

PLATE. I.

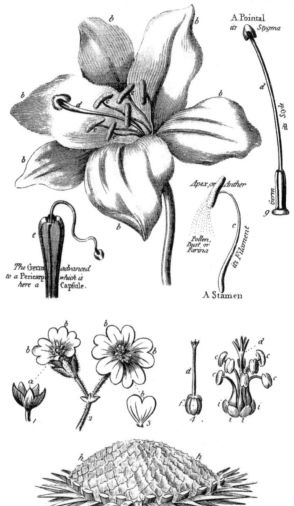

A Pointal

its   Stygma

d'

its Style

g Germ

b

b

d

e

The Germ advanced
to a Pericarp which is
here a Capsule.

Apex, or Anther

Pollen,
Dust, or
Farina

c

its Filament

A Stamen

b   b

b   b

a

b

1   2   3

d'

f

c   c

c   d'

c

i i i

4   i i i

different individual flowers of the fame fpecies,
on feparate plants. I fhall give you as clear a
defcription of thefe feveral parts as I poffibly
can, to enable you to diftinguifh them at firft
fight. The cup, empalement, or calyx (*a*), is that
outer part of the flower, formed of one or more
green, or yellowifh green leaves, fuftaining the
corolla at the bottom, and inclofing it entirely,
before it expands, as you may remark in the
Rofe and Geranium, the latter of which I have
fketched for an illuftration. The empalement is
either

> A cup, as in the polyanthus,
> A fence, as in the hemlock or carrot,
> A catkin, as in the willow or hazle,
> A fheath, as in the narciffus,
> A hufk, as in oats, wheat, or graffes,
> A veil, as in moffes,
> A cap, as in mufhrooms.

The bloffom, petals, or corolla (*b*), is that beautiful coloured part of a flower, which firft draws
the attention, and is regarded by common eyes
as the flower itfelf; but botanifts, more ftrict in
their definitions, appropriate that term to the
compofition of the whole of the fructification, of
which the corolla is only a part.

The threads, or chives, are compofed of two
parts; one long and thin, by which they are

faſtened to the bottom of the corolla, called the filament; the other thicker, placed at the top of the filament, called anthera, or anther. Each anther is a kind of box, which opens when it is ripe, and throws out a yellow duſt, that has a ſtrong ſmell; this is termed pollen or farina, and is the ſubſtance of which bees are ſuppoſed to make their wax. The progreſs of the ſeed to maturity is deſerving the moſt curious attention. Firſt, the calyx opens, then the corolla expands and diſcovers the ſtamens, which generally form a circle within the petals, ſurrounding the pointal. The pollen or duſt, which burſts from the anthers, is abſorbed by the pointal, and paſſing through the ſtyle, reaches the germ, and vivifies the ſeed, which, without this proceſs, would be imperfeƈt and barren. The ſtamens, pointal, and corolla, having performed their reſpeƈtive offices, decline and wither, making room for the ſeed-bud, which daily increaſes, till it attain its perfeƈt ſtate. Many curious experiments have been made by attentive naturaliſts, that prove the neceſſity of this communication between the ſtamens and pointals of the ſame flower, in order to render its ſeeds produƈtive. The ſtamens and pointal being ſometimes diſpoſed on different plants, the trial may be made by ſhutting up a pot of thoſe which have pointals only, in ſome place where they cannot be reached by the

pollen

pollen of the ftamens of other individual plants, and experiment has conftantly fhown, that no feed is produced in this fituation; but how fhall we account for the conveyance of the pollen from one plant to another, growing at a diftance from it? They are both fixed, and cannot approach each other; yet nature, ever abounding in refources, has provided fufficient means for the purpofe. It is probable that there is an attraction between them, which we may imagine, but cannot perceive; this attractive quality may draw the pollen, floating about in the air, as it is wafted by the winds, to the pointals of its own fpecies; or, in many cafes, the numerous tribes of minute winged infects, which we obferve fo bufily employed in a warm day, bafking and hovering upon the flowers, may foon convey this fertilizing duft from one to another, and, whilft they are feafting upon the delicious honey afforded by thefe flowers, return the favour, by rendering them an effential fervice.

The ftyle, pointal, or piftil, is compofed of three parts (Plate I.): the germen, the ftyle, and the ftigma. The germen varies, as to its form, in different plants, but is always placed below the ftyle; its office is to contain the embryo feeds. The ftyle is placed on the germen, and is of a variety of figures and lengths, and fometimes feems wholly wanting. The ftigma alfo

appears

appears of different forms, but always retains the same situation, being invariably placed at the top of the style; or, if that be wanting, it is fixed on the germen.

The seed vessel, or pericarpium, is the germen of the pistil enlarged, as the seeds increase in size, and approach nearer perfection. (Plate I.) The seed vessel is divided into seven kinds:

Capsule, as in poppy and convolvulus,
Pod, as in wallflower and honesty,
Shell, as in pea and broom,
Berry, as in elder and gooseberry,
Fleshy, as in apple and pear,
Pulpy, as in cherry and peach,
Cone, as in fir and pine.

The seeds, or fruit, resemble the eggs of animals, and are the essence of the fruit, containing the rudiments of a new vegetable. The formation of the seed is variously adapted to its purpose, and is composed of several parts: 1st, The heart; this is the principle of life in the future plant, contained within the lobes; it consists of two parts, the plume, which ascends, and forms the future stem; and the beak which descends and becomes the root. 2dly, The side lobes; these supply the heart of the seed with nourishment, till it is capable of extracting support from
the

the earth. In moſt plants the lobes afcend in the form of leaves, and are called feed or radicle leaves; but, in fome, they perifh beneath the furface, without appearing above ground. 3dly, The Scar; is an external mark, where the feed was faſtened within the feed veſſel. 4thly, The feed-coat is a proper cover to fome feeds. It is of various texture and confiſtence in different individuals. Sometimes the feed is crowned with the cup of the flower, and fometimes it is winged with a feather, or with a thin expanded membrane, which aſſiſts the wind to waft or difperfe it to a diſtance. The feed contains the perfeɛt plant in embryo, though, in moſt inſtances, too minute to be difcerned by our organs of fight; but if the feed of a bean or an acorn be fufficiently foaked in warm water, the form of the future plant may be plainly perceived.

The bafe, or receptacle (g), is that part by which the whole fruɛtification is fupported; in many flowers it is not very ſtriking, but in others it is large and remarkable, as in the cotton thiſtle (h). The artichoke will alfo furnifh us with an example: take away the empalement, bloſſoms, and briſtly fubſtances, and the part remaining is the receptacle, which we eat, and call the bottom.

It

It remains for me to defcribe the neêtarium, neêtary, or honey cup, an appendage with which fome flowers are furnifhed, containing a fmall quantity of fweet honey-like juice, from which the bees colleêt their rich treafures. It is very confpicuous in fome flowers, as the nafturtium, crown imperial, columbine, and larkfpur; but lefs vifible in others, and in fome, appears to be entirely wanting. In the dove-footed cranes-bill, there are five yellowifh glands (*i*), which ferve as a neêtary. The ufe is fuppofed to be that of a refervoir, for the nourifhment of the tender feed bud.

I am fearful, my dear fifter, that you are fa-tigued with thefe tedious definitions and defcrip-tions of parts; to me they have been rendered more agreeable, as I have become acquainted with them from vifible objeêts. I hope to participate this pleafure with you in degree, by exemplify-ing them in fome individual flowers, which you may examine by yourfelf; but I fhall defer this till my next letter, and conclude affeêtionately yours

FELICIA.

LETTER

L E T T E R. IV.

Shrubbery, February 24.

THE further I advance in my new study, the more pleasure I take in it, and should value it as an important addition to the number of my in- nocent enjoyments, if partaken with you, my beloved Conflance. Though far separated from each other, I am still desirous of associating with you, as much as the mode of communication will permit, in the delight I feel in examining point- als and stamens. My morning and evening rambles are devoted to this pursuit, nor will Mrs. Snelgrove permit me to pass these hours in mere amusement, but leads me by her amiable reflections, to consider these pleasing objects not only in a botanical view, but by pointing out the peculiar uses of the different parts of their structure, to perceive and admire the proofs of Divine Wisdom exhibited in every leaf, and in every flower; common beholders see these things conflantly without obferving them; how happy am I to have an instructrefs and guide, who teaches me to use my eyes, and exert those faculties which nature has bestowed upon me. The flowers which I have selected as examples,

for

for your examination, to render you perfect
miſtreſs of the parts, are the Crown Imperial, the
Stock Gilliflower, and the Pea ; the laſt, is choſen
on account of the wonderful means uſed in its
conſtruction, for the preſervation of thoſe parts,
neceſſary to perfect the fruit or feed.   They are
not yet in ſeaſon.   The firſt will ſoon appear,
but you muſt wait patiently for the others, till
the time of their blooming arrives, which will
afford you the advantage of watching their progreſs from the firſt appearance of the bud, to the
perfecting the feeds ; nor can you judge accurately of ſeveral of the parts, but by this daily
examination, as they change their form and appearance in different ſtages of the maturity of
the flower.   Gather a crown imperial, as ſoon
as you perceive one blown ; if you obſerve it
cloſely, you will find that it has no cup or empalement ; pull off the beautifully coloured ſcarlet, or ſometimes yellow, petals, which form the
corolla, one by one, and you will find that there
are ſix of them.   The corollas of many flowers
are formed of one petal, as the Canterbury Bell,
and are, on that account, called Monopetalous.
But thoſe that have more petals than one in
their corollas, are termed Polypetalous.   Obſerve a ſort of little column, riſing exactly in
the middle of the corolla, and pointing upwards.
This taken in its whole, is the pointal, but by a
nice

nice infpection, you will find it divided into
three parts: The oblong, three cornered, fwol-
len bafe, which is the germ or ovary, the ftyle
or thread placed upon this, crowned by the ftigma with three notches. Between the pointal
and the corolla, fix other bodies will claim your
notice, which you will readily guefs are the
ftamens, compofed of filaments and anthers.
Continue your vifits to fome other individual
flower of the fame kind, till the petals wither and
fall off, and you will perceive that the germ increafes, and becomes an oblong triangular capfule, within which are flat feeds in three fhells.
Behold the pericarp under the form of this capfule. I had like to have forgotten to mention
the honey-cup, which may be found at the bottom of the petals, in the form of a little hole.
The willow wren creeps up the ftems of this
plant, and fips the drops of honey as they hang
from the petals. After having carried you
through the various parts of a Crown Imperial,
I will introduce a Stock Gilliflower to your ac-
quaintance, which, I hope, will afford you as
much entertainment as the flower already examined. It is neceffary that I fhould remark,
that our ftock muft be a fingle one. Thofe fine
purple double ftocks that we prized fo highly
laft fummer, would have been totally difregarded by a botanical ftudent, who confiders all
double

double flowers, either as the fport of nature, or the effect of art, and confequently improper for his invefligation. In the examination of this flower, the firft thing that you will fee is the ca- lyx, an exterior part, which was wanting in the Crown Imperial. In the ftock, it confifts of four pieces, which we muft call leaves, leaflets, or folioles, having no proper name to exprefs them by, as we have of petals for the pieces that com- pofe the corolla. Thefe leaflets are commonly unequal by pairs. That is, there are two oppo- fite and equal, of a fmaller fize, and two others alfo oppofite and equal, but larger. This calyx contains a corolla, compofed of four petals. I fay nothing of their colour, becaufe that makes no permanent part of their character. Each of thefe petals is faftened to the receptacle, or bot- tom of the calyx, by a narrow pale part, called the claw of the petal, and this fpreads out over the top of the calyx, into a large, flat, coloured piece, diftinguifhed by the name of lamina, or the border. Admire the regularity of the corolla of the flowers of this tribe. The petals grow generally wide of each other, and exactly oppo- fite to one another, forming a figure refembling that of a crofs, which has given them the name of cruciform, or crofs-fhaped. The petals of the corolla, and the leaflets of the calyx are fitu- ated alternately; and this pofition prevails in all

flowers,

flowers, in which is a correspondent number of petals and leaflets. In the centre of the corolla is one piftil or pointal, long and cylindric, chiefly compofed of a germ, ending in a very fhort ftyle, and that terminated by an oblong ftigma, which is bifed, or divided into two parts, that are bent back on each fide. It remains now to fpeak of the ftamens; there are fix of them, two, fhorter than the other four, oppofite to each other, thefe are feparated by the reft, as are alfo the others in pairs. When the corolla withers, the germ grows confiderably in length, and thickens a little as the fruit ripens; when it is ripe, it becomes a kind of flat pod, called fi-lique. This filique is compofed of two valves, each covering a fmall cell, and thefe cells are divided by a thin partition. When the feeds are ripe, the valves open from the bottom up-wards, to give them paffage, and remain faft to the ftigma at top. Then you may difcover the flat round feeds ranged along each fide of the partition, and you will find that they are faftened alternately, to right and left, by a fhort pedicle, or footftalk, to the futures or edges of the par-tition. The great number of fpecies in this clafs, has determined botanifts to divide it into two fe&tions, in which the flowers are perfe&ly alike; but there is a material difference in the fruits, pericarps, or feed veffels. The defcription
of

of the Pea, will enlarge my letter to an unreafonable length, and as I am tired, and fuppofe that
you muſt be fo likewife, I will defer it to my
next. Adieu, dear fiſter; fay every thing for
me, to my aunt and coufins, that is kind and affectionate, and believe me me ever your

FELICIA.

LETTER V.

Shrubbery, March 1.

IT is with renewed pleafure I devote the prefent half hour to your fervice, fince you affure
me, that my letters contribute to your amufement, and that you purfue the fame object, that
occupies me daily, from the hints I have given
you. I wiſh you had a better guide, that could
fatisfy your enquiries, and animate your induf-
try by fuperior ſkill; affection and a defire to
pleafe, will ſtimulate me to repeat Mrs. Snelgrove's lectures accurately: I wiſh I may be able
to give you a clear idea of what I defcribe; but
I find it difficult to exprefs forms and ſhapes by
writing.

writing. I believe I fhall be obliged to have fre-
quent recourfe to my pencil, which will reprefent,
in a more lively manner, the pleafing objects of
our prefent refearches. In order to affift you in
the examination of the minute parts of fmall
flowers, it will be neceffary to provide a magnifying glafs, a needle, lancet, and a pair of fmall
fciffars, to render the diffecting them eafier; for
many of their parts are too delicate to be handl-
ed, for which reafon a pair of fmall nippers will
be an ufeful addition to the inftruments, that I
have already named. Although I have wandered far from the fubject, I have not forgotten my
promife, of defcribing the curious mechanifm
employed in the ftructure of the pea flower.

On examining this elegant and wonderful
bloffom, you will obferve that the calyx is of
one piece, divided at the edge into five fegments,
or diftinct points, two of which are wider than
the other three, and are fituated on the upper
fide of the calyx, whilft the three narrower ones
occupy the lower part. The corolla is compofed of four petals, the firft is broad and large,
covering the others, and ftanding, as it were, on
the upper-part of the corolla, to defend and fhel-
ter it from the injuries of the weather, in the
manner of a fhield; by way of pre-eminence, it
is called the Standard, or Banner. In taking off
the ftandard, remark how deeply it is inferted on
each

each fide, that it may not eafily be driven out of
its place by the wind. The fide petals, diftinguifhed by the name of wings, are expofed to
view by taking off the banner. They are as
ufeful in protecting the fides of the flower, as
the banner is in covering the whole. Take off
the wings, and you will perceive the keel, called
fo on account of its fancied refemblance to the
fhape of the bottom of a boat; this inclofes and
preferves the centre of the flower from harm,
which its delicate texture might receive from
air and water. If you are curious to examine
the contents of this little cafket, flip the keel
gently down, and you will difcover a membrane,
terminated by ten diftinct threads, which furround the germ, or embryo of the legume or
pod. Each of thefe threads or filaments is
tipped with a yellow anther, the farina of which
covers the ftigma, which terminates the ftyle, or
grows along the fide of it. The filaments form
an additional defence to the germ, from external
injuries. As the other parts decay and fall off,
the germ gradually becomes a legume or pod.
This legume is diftinguifhed from the filique of
the cruciform tribe, by the feeds being faftened
to one fide only of the cafe or fhell, though alternately to each valve of it. Compare the pod
of a pea and a ftock together, and you will immediately perceive the difference. The footftalk
which

which fupports this flower is flender, and eafily
moved by the wind. In wet and ftormy weather, the pea turns its back to the ftorm, whilft
the banner unfolds the wings, by clofing about
them, and partly covers them; they perform the
fame office to the keel, containing the effential
parts of the fructification. Thus is this flower
curioufly fheltered and defended from its natural enemies, rain and wind; and, when the
ftorm is over, and fair weather returns, the
flower changes its pofition, as if fenfible of the
alteration, expands its wings, and erects its ftandard as before. Wonderful are the means of
prefervation ufed by the all-wife Creator to defend the tender and important parts of the fructification of plants from injury; but he feems to
have provided, in an efpecial manner, for the fe-
curity of thofe, which ferve as nourifhment to men
and animals, as does the greater part of the leguminous or pulfe kind. I imagine, by this time,
that you are pretty well acquainted with the feveral parts that compofe a flower, and would recognife them, though in an individual that was an
utter ftranger to you. Confirm your knowledge
by practice, and do not fuffer a day to pafs without amufing yourfelf in diffecting fome flower
or other. When you are perfectly acquainted
with this entrance of the fcience, Mrs. Snelgrove fays, that I may proceed to give you a

C

fketch

sketch of the arrangement and classification of plants, for it is by method only, that it is possible to obtain a knowledge of so many particulars. Botany would be indeed a most fatiguing and almost unattainable science, were we obliged to learn the peculiarities of every plant, one by one; but the difficulty ceases, or at least is greatly diminished, by classing those together, in which there is a similarity in some one point. Eminent naturalists have at different times exerted their talents to perform this task. Tournefort is a name that was highly distinguished on this list, before the time of Linnæus, whose superior genius has raised him above all his predecessors : his system is now universally adopted. As it will furnish matter for several letters, I shall not enlarge upon it at this time. but proceed to relate some anecdotes concerning this great man, that I think likely to afford you entertainment. Charles Linnæus was a native of Sweden, and the son of an obscure clergyman in that country : his father was a great admirer of the vegetable productions of nature, and adorned the environs of his rural mansion with the natural produce of the neighbouring fields. Young Linnæus caught the enthusiasm, and early imbibed the same taste, with such warmth, that he was never able to bend his mind to any other pursuit. His father intended to bring him up to the church, but he shewed

such

fuch a diflike to theological ftudies, to which
his nature was averfe, that his relations, angry
and difappointed at his want of application, by
way of punifhment, purpofed to bind him appren-
tice to a fhoe-maker; but an over-ruling Providence deftined him to fill a more noble and diftinguifhed walk in life. A phyfician, named Roth-
man, obferving him to be a lad of genius, com-
paffionated his fituation, and relieved him from
it, by taking him into his own family, and in-
ftructing him in the fcience of medicine. By
accident he lent him Tournefort's Elements of
Botany to read, which renewed his former tafte
for the productions of Flora, and decided the
caft of his future character. From that time he
devoted all his leifure to his favourite ftudy, and
by the luftre of his abilities, drew the attention
of fome of the moft learned men in Europe,
who encouraged and patronifed him in the pro-
fecution of that amiable and interefting purfuit,
to which he had devoted himfelf. Botany was
in an imperfect ftate, when he undertook to
form a new fyftem, which he effected fo excel-
lently, that it has immortalifed his name, and
although it may probably receive improvement
from fome future naturalift, it is never likely to
be fuperfeded. The ftudies of Linnæus were
not wholly confined to botany. He formed the
prefent claffification of moft other branches of

natural

natural hiſtory, and, by his judicious arrange-
ments, has rendered the acquiſition of the knowledge of nature eaſier to the ſtudent, than it was
before his ſyſtem was invented.   It is late, and
I am obliged to lay aſide my pen.—Farewel.

FELICIA.

LETTER VI.

DEAR SISTER,   *Shrubbery, March 6.*

I AM fearful, leſt by this time, you are wearied
with the minute deſcriptions of the ſeparate
parts of flowers and plants, and that you begin
to wiſh for ſomething more amuſing.   Botany,
like all other ſciences, has its elements, which
muſt be patiently learned by the pupil, before
ſufficient knowledge can be attained, to enjoy
the moſt pleaſing parts of it.   I have already
hinted the neceſſity of forming ſome ſyſtem,
that may reduce the innumerable individuals of
the vegetable kingdom, to the compaſs of human memory and comprehenſion.   All the
known vegetable produ&ions, upon the ſurface
of

of the globe, have been reduced by naturalifts to Claffes, Orders, Genera, Species, and Varieties. The Claffes are compofed of Orders; the Orders are compofed of Genera; the Genera of Species; and the Species of Varieties. Let us endeavour to attain a clearer idea of Claffes, Orders, &c. by comparing them with the general divifions of the inhabitants of the earth.

Vegetables refemble Man,
Claffes, Nations of Men,
Orders, Tribes, or Divifions of Nations,
Genera, the Families that compofe the Tribes,
Species, Individuals of which Families confift,
Varieties, Individuals under different appearances.

Do not think, dear fifter, that I am capable of methodifing fo accurately, without the kind affiftance of one, who fuperintends my letters, and points out what I fhould write; it is not neceffary to fay, that Mrs. Snelgrove is that attentive affectionate friend, who will not allow me to do any thing without fome degree of regularity. Many great men, as I told you in my laft, have formed fyftems after different plans. Thofe of Tournefort and Linnæus are moft efteemed; both are ingenious : but as that of Linnæus has fuperfeded all others, it will not be

neceffary

neceſſary to confound your memory with any
other, his being the one univerſally adopted; it
is that in which it is proper to be completely in-
ſtructed.

Linnæus, diſſatisfied with every ſyſtem invented before his time, undertook to form a new
one, upon a plan approaching nearer to perfection, and depending on parts leſs liable to varia-
tion. The ſtamens and pointals are the baſis of
his claſſification. He has divided all vegetables
into twenty-four claſſes. Theſe claſſes are ſubdi-
vided into nearly one hundred orders; theſe orders
include about two thouſand families or genera; and
theſe families about twenty thouſand ſpecies, beſides the innumerable varieties produced by the accidental changes of cultivation, ſoil, and climate.
As you have acquired accurate notions of ſtamens
and piſtils, you will find but little difficulty in
making yourſelf miſtreſs of the claſſes and orders; the former depending principally upon
the number, the length, the connection, or the
ſituation of the ſtamens; the latter are diſtinguiſhed by the number, or other circumſtances
of the pointals. The characters of the genera
are marked from ſome particulars in the flower,
unnoticed in the definitions of the claſſes or
orders. The generic deſcription includes *all*
the moſt obvious appearances in the flower. In
a ſcience depending ſo much on memory, and
                                        minute

minute definitions, it is advifable to procced
ftep by ftep, and make yourfelf perfectly acquainted with the claffes, before you advance to
the orders. Should you gather a flower, in order
to know to what clafs it belongs, obferve firft,
whether it be a perfect flower, containing both
ftamens and pointals; if that be the cafe, examine whether the ftamens are entirely feparate
from the pointal, and each other, from top to
bottom. If you find that they are perfectly diftinct, and of equal height when at maturity, and
not fo many as twenty, the number of them
alone will be fufficient to determine the clafs.

Thofe that have one ftamen will belong to the
firft clafs, Monandria.
Thofe that have two, to the fecond, Diandria.
Thofe that have three, to the third, Triandria.
Thofe that have four, to the fourth, Tetran-
dria.
Thofe that have five, to the fifth, Pentandria.
Thofe that have fix, to the fixth, Hexandria.
Thofe that have feven, to the feventh, Hep-
tandria.
Thofe that have eight, to the eighth, Octan-
dria.
Thofe that have nine, to the ninth, Ennean-
dria.
Thofe that have ten, to the tenth, Decandria.

C 4   Thus

Thus far, it is eafy to arrange each flower under its proper clafs, as you have nothing farther
to do, but obferve the four above-mentioned peculiarities, and to count the ftamens, and refer
them to their refpective claffes, according to their
number. The following claffes depend upon other
diftinctions, which I fhall enumerate in their proper order. The names of the claffes are compofed of two Greek words, ingenioufly contrived to exprefs the peculiarities of each clafs, and
abfolutely neceffary to be learned perfectly by
heart, which cannot be confidered as a difficult
tafk, as there are but twenty-four of them, and far
the greater number terminate in the fame word,
andria.

Flowers growing wild, without culture, are the
moft fuitable for examination, becaufe thofe that
are domefticated in the rich foil of our gardens,
are frequently transformed into fomething very
different from what nature made them, by
change of nourifhment, &c. It will be proper
to extend your obfervation to feveral flowers of
the fame clafs, as it fometimes happens, that the
number of the ftamens varies from accidental
caufes. But there is a beautiful regularity in
moft of Nature's works, that may affift you on
this occafion. If the calyx of your flower be
divided into five fegments, and the corolla be
formed of five petals, or divided into five parts,
                                                            although

although you find fix or feven ftamens, it is
more than probable, that, on further infpection,
you will find that it belongs to the fifth clafs,
Pentandria. It is time to conclude this digref-
fion, and proceed to the eleventh clafs, Dode-
candria, or twelve ftamens. Some flowers in
this clafs contain fewer, and others more, than
the fpecified number. All plants are included
in it, that have any number of ftamens from
eleven to nineteen inclufive, provided they are
difunited. Let us fearch then, for fome more
invariable characteriftics to diftinguifh this clafs,
and we fhall find that the ftamens are all fixed
to the bafe or receptacle. In the twelfth clafs,
Icofandria, there fhould be twenty ftamens, or
nearly that number, ftanding upon the fides of
the cup, and fometimes partly on the bloffom;
whereas the former and the following claffes are
marked by their ftanding on the receptacle. Obferve, as an additional diftinction of this clafs
from the next, that the cup confifts of one concave leaf, and that the petals are likewife fixed
by their claws to the fides of the cup.

Many ftamens, from twenty to any number,
are found in the thirteenth clafs, Polyandria,
fixed on the bafe or receptacle. The flowers of
this clafs have either a calyx, confifting of feveral folioles, or none at all.

C 5

In the preceding claſſes, no attention has been
paid to the length of the ſlamens, but they
have been ſuppoſed to be all nearly equal in
that reſpeſt.   The diſtinſtive marks of the next
two claſſes depend chiefly on that circumſtance.

The fourteenth claſs, Didynamia, or two pow-
ers, will preſent you with flowers containing four
ſtamens, ranged in one row, the inner pair ſhorter
than the outer one.   The eſſential marks of
this claſs conſiſt in the proportionable arrangement of four ſtamens, as I have already expreſſ-
ed, accompanied with one pointal, and inveſted
with an irregular Monopetalous corolla.   Thoſe
flowers that are called labiate, or lip-ſhaped, as
well as the perſonate, or maſked flowers, are
included in this claſs; thoſe of the firſt kind,
have two lips, the one projeſting over the other,
forming, as it were, a ſhelter to the parts of the
fruſtification from rain, &c.   The lips are generally cloſed in the perſonate corollas, and entirely conceal the ſlamen and pointal from ſight.

Claſs the fifteenth, Tetradynamia; the mean-
ing of this long word, is the power or ſuperiority
of four, and accordingly its charaſter is diſtinguiſhed by ſix ſtamens, four of which are long,
and the remaining two are ſhort.   It is chiefly
compoſed of croſs-ſhaped flowers, with which
you are already pretty well acquainted.   The
five following claſſes are not diſtinguiſhed by
the

the number of the ſtamens, but by their ſituation. Their union or adheſion, either by their anthers or their filaments, to the pointal, decides to which of them they belong.

The ſixteenth claſs, Monodelphia, or one brotherhood. In this claſs the filaments are united at the bottom, but ſeparate at the top, as in the Marſh Mallow tribe.

The ſeventeenth claſs, Diadelphia, or two brotherhoods. The filaments of theſe flowers are alſo united at bottom, not into one bundle or brotherhood, but into two; and conſiſts of the papilionaceous flowers, which contain ten ſtamens and one pointal, nine of the ſtamens form one bundle below, the remaining one and the pointal form another above.

The eighteenth claſs, Polyadelphia, or many brotherhoods. The filaments in this claſs are united at the bottom only, into three or more bundles or brotherhoods.

The nineteenth claſs, Syngyneſia, is compoſed of flowers, generally compound, the eſſential character of which conſiſts in the lips being united, ſo as to form a cylinder; and a ſingle ſeed being placed upon the receptacle under each floret, perhaps, an example will give you the cleareſt idea of a compound flower; the Thiſtle is one ready at hand, being compoſed of ſmall flowers or florets, ſitting upon a common

C 6 receptacle

receptacle, and inclofed by one common empalement.

The twentieth clafs, Gynandria. Many ftamens attached to, and growing upon the pointal itfelf. Hitherto our attention has been confined to fuch flowers only as are termed complete, having both ftamens and pointals on the fame flower. But the next three claffes will furnifh us with examples of thofe which have only the one or the other in the fame flower.

The twenty-firft clafs, Monœcia, or one houfe. The flowers of different kinds being produced in the fame habitation, or on the fame individual plant. But in the next, or twenty-fecond clafs, Diœcia, or two houfes. The different kinds of flowers, which are diftinguifhed by the names ftaminiferous, or ftamen bearing, and piftilliferous, or bearing piftils, are produced by different trees or plants of the fame fpecies.

The twenty-third clafs, Polygamia, provides for the only remaining cafe that can poffibly happen, and confifts of flowers with ftamens and pointals in feparate flowers, as well as both in the fame flower, or one on different plants.

The twenty-fourth clafs, Cryptogamia. Plants, whofe flowers are not perceptible by the naked eye, though there is good reafon to believe, that no plant exifts without the effential parts that conftitute the flower. The loweft kinds of
vegetables

TABLE OF THE CLASSES, referring to Plate IV.

	Class.		Examples.	Fig.
1	Monandria.	One Stamen.	Madder,	1
2	Diandria.	Two Stamens.	Speedwell,	2
3	Triandria.	Three Stamens.	Grasses,	3
4	Tetrandria.	Four Stamens. (All of the same length)	Teasel,	4
5	Pentandria.	Five Stamens. (Anthers not united)	Honeysuckle,	5
6	Hexandria.	Six Stamens. (All of the same length)	Hyacinth,	6
7	Heptandria.	Seven Stamens.	Wintergreen,	7
8	Octandria.	Eight Stamens.	Mezereon,	8
9	Enneandria.	Nine Stamens.	Gladiole,	9
10	Decandria.	Ten Stamens. (Threads not united)	Pink,	10
11	Dodecandria.	Twelve Stamens, or more. (Fixed to the Receptacle)	Houseleek,	11
12	Icosandria.	Twenty Stamens. (Fixed upon the Calyx or Corolla)	Strawberry,	12
13	Polyandria.	Many Stamens. (Fixed to the Receptacle)	Poppy,	13
14	Didynamia.	Four Stamens, two longer. One Pointal. Flowers ringent.	Foxglove,	14
15	Tetradynamia.	Six Stamens, four longer. One Pointal. Flowers cruciform.	Stock Gillflower,	15
16	Monadelphia.	Threads united at bottom, but separate at top.	Rose Mallow,	16
17	Diadelphia.	Threads in two sets. Flowers Butterfly-shaped.	Everlasting Pea,	17
18	Polyadelphia.	Threads in many sets; in three or more sets.	St. John's Wort,	18
19	Syngenesia.	Anthers united. Five Stamens. One Pointal. Flowers compound.	Dandelion,	19
20	Gynandria.	Stamens upon the Pointal.	Orchis,	20
21	Monoecia.	Stamens and Pointals in separate Flowers, upon the same Plant.	Cucumber,	21
22	Dioecia.	Stamens and Pointals different, upon different Plants.	Hop,	22
23	Polygamia.	Various situations. Stamens only, Pointals only, or perfect Flowers.	Ash,	23
24	Cryptogamia.	Flowers inconspicuous.	Ferns, Moss, Liverwort, Mushrooms,	24

a distinguishes the Stamens; b the Pointals.

To face Letter VII.

The material originally positioned here is too large for reproduction in this reissue. A PDF can be downloaded from the web address given on page iv of this book, by clicking on 'Resources Available'.

PLATE.IV.

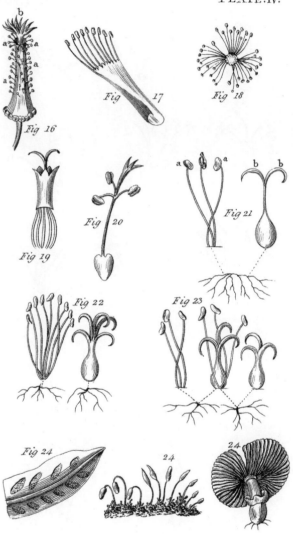

Fig 16

Fig 17

Fig 18

Fig 19

Fig 20

Fig 21

Fig 22

Fig 23

Fig 24

24

24

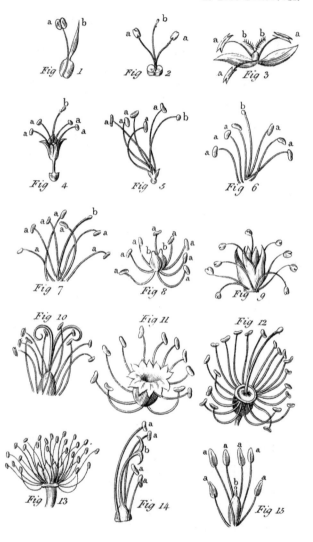

Fig 1

Fig 2

Fig 3

Fig 4

Fig 5

Fig 6

Fig 7

Fig 8

Fig 9

Fig 10

Fig 11

Fig 12

Fig 13

Fig 14

Fig 15

vegetables are the objects of this clafs, as Ferns, Moffes, Sea Weeds or Thongs, and Fungufes.

To thefe twenty-four claffes, Linnæus has added the Palm trees, which do not fall under the defcription of any of the claffes. He calls them Princes of India, bearing their fructification on a fpadia or receptacle, within a fpathe or fheath. Remarkable for their prodigious height, diftinguifhed by an unvaried, undivided, perennial trunk, crowned at top by an evergreen tuft of leaves, and rich in abundance of large fine fruit. But fince the time that Linnæus wrote, more certain knowledge of them has been obtained, and many of them are arranged in the fixth clafs. If you have patience and perfeverance to learn the contents of this letter, you will deferve to be chofen queen of the May.

FELICIA.

LETTER VII.

Shrubbery, March 26.

I HAVE been in no hafte to burden you, my dear Conftance, with another letter, till I thought that I had given you time for digefting the laft,

the

the fubject of which is too important to the fcience in which you are engaged, to be flightly paffed over. When you find yourfelf perfect in your knowledge of the claffes, or larger divifions, this letter is intended to fupply you with frefh employment, by making the diftinctions of the orders that compofe them. The orders of the firft thirteen claffes are founded wholly on the number of the pointals, fo that, by adding *gynia*, inftead of *andria*, to the Greek words fignifying the numbers, you will eafily obtain a knowledge of them, as Monogynia, one pointal ; Digynia, two pointals ; Trigynia, three pointals ; Tetragynia, four pointals, and fo on. In thofe cafes, where the pointals have no apparent ftyles, the ftigmas are to be numbered, which generally adhere to the capfule like fmall protuberances, as may be obferved in the flowers of the Poppy.

There is no occafion to count the pointals in the fourteenth clafs, Dydinamia, becaufe all the flowers of the Ringent tribe, including both the labiate and perfonate flowers, have but one pointal : but there is another obvious difference that prefents itfelf, as an affiftant in difcriminating the orders of this clafs, for moft of the plants, that have a labiate flower, have four naked feeds at the bottom of the calyx, and the perfonate flowers are fucceeded by a capfule, containing many fmall feeds. From this diftinction arifes

an

an elegant, eafy, and natural divifion of the
fourteenth clafs into two orders; Gymnofpermia, comprehending fuch as have naked feeds ;
and Angiofpermia, confifting of thofe that have
their feeds covered, or inclofed in a capfule.
The fruit fupplies us with marks for the fubdivifion of the next clafs, Tetradynamia, in which
the flowers alfo have but one pointal. It is divided into two orders, called Siliculofa and Siliquofa, from the form of the fruit, which is denominated Silide and Silique. The plants of
the firft order have a filide, or fhort roundifh
feed-veffel, or pericarp. Thofe of the fecond,
contain their feeds in a filique, or long flender
pod. In the fixteenth, feventeenth, and eighteenth claffes, the orders are diftinguifhed by
the number of the ftamens.

The chief difficulty, with refpect to the orders, lies in the clafs Syngenefia. This clafs
comprehends thofe flowers that are called compound, of which I gave you fome notion in
treating of the claffes. Now, if you examine
thefe flofcules, or florets, nicely, you will perceive that they have fometimes both ftamens and
pointal ; but you will alfo difcover, that fome
have ftamens only, whilft others are furnifhed with
a pointal alone ; and laftly, that there are flofcules without either the one or the other. Let us
diftinguifh the firft of thefe, by the term perfect
flofcules

flofcules; the fecond by that of ftaminiferous;
the third we will call piftilliferous; and the
fourth neuter flofcules. Thefe variations require exaɛ attention, becaufe on them, and on
the form of the florets, Linnæus has founded
the four firft orders of this clafs. Polygamia is
the family name applied to all the orders, except
the laft; it is ufed in oppofition to Monogamia,
Πολυς fignifying many, and μονος one, and implies
that there are many florets inclofed within one
common calyx, which coincides with the idea
of a compound flower. The firft order is called
Polygamia Æqualis; the peculiar name æqualis
means regular or equal, and infers that the flofcules are fimilar, and all furnifhed with both
ftamens and pointals, as in the Dandelion. In
the fecond order, Polygamia Superflua, all the
florets of the difk, or centre of the flower, are
perfeɛ; thofe of the ray or circumference,
piftilliferous, both of them produce feed: the
Daify is a familiar inftance. The third order of
the clafs, Syngynefia, is entitled Polygamia Fruf-
tranea. The florets in the difk or centre are
perfeɛ, and produce feed, whilft thofe of the
ray are imperfeɛ, and therefore fruftrate or
barren; from which circumftance the order
takes its name; example, Bluebottle. The fituation is reverfed in the fourth order, Polygamia
Neceffaria; for the florets in the difk, though
apparently

apparently perfect, are not really fo, and therefore produce no perfect feed; but the fertility
of the piftilliferous flofcules in the ray compenfate for the deficiency of thofe in the centre of
the flower, as is feen in the Marygold. The
fifth order, Polygamia Segrata, has many flofcules inclofed in one common calyx, yet each of
the flofcules has one appropriate to itfelf. Globe
Thiftle fupplies me with a beautiful example.
Monogamia, the fixth and laft order, confifts of
plants, with fimple, not compound, flowers,
which peculiarity will fufficiently diftinguifh it
from the reft, remembering at the fame time to
attend to its claffical character, of having the
ftamens united by the anthers : this order is exemplified in the Violets. The orders of the
three following claffes, Gynandria, Monœcia,
and Diœcia, being founded upon the ftamens,
and taking their names from the preceding
claffes, according to the number, union, or dif-
union of the ftamens in the refpective flowers,
require no particular elucidation.

There are three orders in the twenty-third
clafs, Polygamia, depending upon the mode in
which the three forts of flowers may be arranged.
When a plant bears both perfect and imperfect
flowers, the order is entitled Monœcia. But
when they are produced on feparate plants of
the fame fpecies, the order is Diœcia. And
when

when one plant of the fame kind produces perfect flowers, a fecond ftaminiferous flowers, and
a third piftilliferous flowers, the order is known
by the name of Triœcia, or three houfes; imply-
ing that the three forts of flowers have three different habitations.

The laft clafs, Cryptogamia, confifts of plants,
whofe parts of fructification are either obfcure
or very minute, which prevents the poffibility
of arranging the orders according to the number
and fituation of the ftamens and pointals. The
peculiarity of ftructure of the plants of this clafs,
diftinguifhes them fufficiently from all others:
It is naturally divided into four orders: firft
Filices, or Ferns; fecond, Mufci, or Mofles;
third, Algæ, or Sea Weeds; and fourth, Fungi,
or Fungufes. The ferns comprehend all plants
that bear their feeds in the back, or edges of the
leaf. The mofs kind forms the fecond order.
The third includes the lichens, fuci, and many
others, whofe effential parts are too minute or
obfcure for inveftigation. If the fungufes have
any fructification, it is imagined to be underneath, in the gills, pores, &c. Thus we have,
at length, reached the end of the claffes and orders, which I think will fupply our walks with
amufement for the whole fummer; and, by
forming a tafte for this delightful part of nature,
lay a foundation that will continue to furnifh
                                                    new

new and interesting objects, to the end of our
lives. I cannot wonder that a country residence
is disagreeable to those, who have no relish for
the objects it presents; but it may well be preferred by persons of true taste and observation,
who clearly perceive the traces of Infinite Wisdom and Intelligence in the structure of every
leaf and every blossom. May rural pleasures always suffice to render you cheerful and happy.

FELICIA.

LETTER VIII.

Shrubbery, April 2.

WHENEVER you set out on a botanical
excursion, remember to put your magnifying
glass and dissecting instruments into your pocket,
that you may not be obliged to neglect those
flowers that are small, for want of this precaution. Always gather several flowers of the same
kind, if possible, some just opening, and others
with the seed-vessels almost ripe; and as I in-
tend to select our examples from plants of British
growth,

growth, you muſt feek for them growing wild
in their native fields ; nor confine your walks
within the limits of a garden wall. Thus I
hope you will obtain health, and a knowledge of
vegetables at the ſame time. That nothing
might be left undone by Linnæus, the great
maſter of method and arrangement, to render the
acquiſition of his favourite ſcience eaſy, he has
divided the orders, when numerous, into ſeveral
diviſions, each including one or more genera,
which is a means of diminiſhing the pupil's labour. Let us ſuppoſe, that you have a plant
under obſervation, belonging to an order that
contains a great number of genera : you are con-
fuſed, and know not to which to apply it. But
on remarking theſe diviſions, you are enabled
to place it among a few of its brethren, there
remains but little difficulty to diſcover its peculiar marks, and aſſure yourſelf of the identi-
cal plant. The firſt claſs, Monandria, contains
but two orders, both depending upon the number of the pointals. Moſt of theſe plants are
natives of India. Our ditches and muddy ponds,
however, produce one example, that you may
eaſily procure. It is called Mareſtail (Hippuris)
has neither empalement nor bloſſom. Its ſingle
ſtamen grows upon the receptacle, terminated
by an anther ſlightly cloven, behind which you
will find the pointal, with its awl-ſhaped ſtigma,
tapering

tapering to a point. The ftem is ftraight, and
jointed, and the leaves grow in whorls round the
joints; at the bafe of each leaf is a flower, fo
that the number of flowers and leaves is equal.
Its feafon of flowering is the month of May.
As there are but few objefts of native growth
to arreft our attention in this clafs, we will proceed to the next.

The Privet (Ligiftrum) is a fhrub common
enough in the hedges in many parts of England,
and when mixed with other fhrubs, makes a
pleafing variety in our gardens. It bears a
white bloffom, and generally flowers in June.
It has a very fmall tubular calyx of one leaf, its
rim divided into four parts. The bloffom is alfo
monopetalous, and funnel-fhaped, with an expanded border, cut into four egg-fhaped fegments. Its ftamens are two, which determine
it to belong to this clafs, placed oppofite to each
other, and nearly as long as the bloffom. The
feed-bud is roundifh, the ftyle fhort, terminated
by a thick, blunt, cloven ftigma. The feed-
veffel is a black berry, containing but one cell,
which inclofes four feeds. The leaves grow in
pairs, and are fometimes variegated with white
or yellow ftripes. The berries are ufeful to
the dyers, as they give a durable green colour
to filk or wool by the addition of alum. In the
fecond divifion of this order is a genus, the

Latin

Latin name of which is Veronica, but commonly known by that of Speedwell. There are a
great many ſpecies of it, which has induced
Linnæus to treat it in the ſame manner as the
orders, and to divide it into three principal diviſions. Firſt, Flowers growing in ſpikes. Se-
condly, Flowers in broad bunches. Thirdly,
Fruit-ſtalks with one flower. The monopetalous wheel-ſhaped corolla, divided into four ſegments, the loweſt of which is narrower than the
reſt, and that oppoſite to it the broadeſt, eaſily
diſtinguiſh this genus, as well as the heart-ſhaped
flatted capſule with two cells. Several of the
ſpecies are cultivated, and increaſe the beauty of
the flower beds in the early part of ſummer.
You will ſoon be tired of theſe deſcriptions, if
you do not unite them to the living objeƈts.
Search for ſome others in the ſame claſſes, and
oblige me with your account of them. In this
manner we may contribute to each others amuſement, though we cannot enjoy each others company. Yours, with warm affeƈtion,

FELICIA.

LETTER

LETTER IX.

Shrubbery, April 15.

HOW often have we walked through the meadows and paſtures, without opening our eyes to the wonders they contain! We were, indeed, delighted with gathering a bouquet of the gayeſt flowers we could colleﬅ, and ſometimes admitted a piece of graſs, for the beauty of its pendant head. But we little thought, that every ſingle blade of theſe apparently inſignificant plants, as we have been accuſtomed to conſider them, bears a diſtinﬅ flower, perfeﬅ in all its parts; nay, more complete than the fragrant Lily or the gaudy Tulip, and only requires to be nicely viewed, to excite our value and admiration. This humble tribe is extremely numerous, and, like modeſt merit in other ſituations, of moſt extenſive utility. There are upwards of three hundred ſpecies, but as they have been ſcarcely noticed till within twenty or thirty years, we may believe that time will improve our knowledge of their properties and ſtruﬅure. Dr. Withering ſays, " that, the leaves furniſh paſturage for cattle, the ſmaller ſeeds are food for birds, and the larger for man; but ſome
are

are preferred to others : as the Fefcue for fheep;
the Meadowgrafs for cows; the Canary for
fmall birds ; the Oat for horfes ; the Ryegrafs,
Barley, and Wheat for men ; befides, a variety
of beautiful infects derive their nourifhment
from them :" and if we enumerate the remote
benefits that accrue from them, their confe-
quence increafes to an extraordinary height.
What may be called the moft important articles
of both food and clothing, are derived from this
unnoticed and neglected tribe. Bread, meat,
beer, milk, butter, cheefe, leather, and wool, and
all the advantages produced from the ufe of cattle, would be loft without them.

But I think I hear my dear fifter exclaim,
you are very earneft in fetting forth the praifes
of graffes, and, in order to enhance their dignity,
you rank the various kinds of corn among them.
But you will foon be convinced, when I have.
given you their general character, that they are
all of one family. Obferve their whole appearance : you know a blade of corn or grafs, at firft
fight, from every other plant that grows near
them. What is it that diftinguifhes them ?
Their fimple, ftraight, unbranched ftalk, hollow
and jointed, commonly called a ftraw, with long,
narrow, tapering leaves, placed at each knob or
joint of the ftalk, and fheathing or inclofing it,
as if by way of fupport : their ears or heads.
                                    confift

confift of a hufk, generally compofed of two
valves, which form the empalement, the larger
leaflet hollow, the fmaller flat, within which is,
what may be termed the bloffom, which is alfo a
hufk of two valves, dry and fhining: thefe minute flowers are furnifhed with a honey-cup,
but it requires very good eyes or a glafs to dif-
cern it. The fruﬁification of graffes is beft obferved, when they are nearly ripe, and their
hufks expanded, which renders their three flender filaments, tipped with large oblong double
anthers, eafily perceptible: thefe filaments play
freely about upon the flighteft motion, and their
number, three, will leave you at no lofs to place
thefe plants in the third clafs, Triandria; and
the two pointals, reflefted or turned back, with
their feathered ftigmas, determine them to belong to the fecond order of that clafs: feed-
veffel they have none, but each feed is inclofed,
either by the bloffom or empalement. As they
ripen, the hufks open, and, if not timely gathered, the feed falls to the ground, which is one
among many means ufed for the increafe and
propagation of vegetables. They have fibrous
roots, fomething like a bundle of ftrings. The
extraordinary precautions difplayed in the prefervation of thofe plants, that are chiefly deftined to fuftain men and animals, was remarked in
the delineation of the papilionaceous tribe; and

D   here

here again the fame care is confpicuous, and
calls for further gratitude and admiration. What
a dreary habitation would this earth be, were it
deftitute of its verdant covering, fo foft to our
feet, and refrefhing to our fight! But when we
reflect, that this delightful carpet, which is
fpread every where around us, is the prey of
almoft every animal that approaches it, how
much is to be apprehended for its fafety. But
Providence has ordained, with the utmoft wifdom and beneficence, that the more the leaves
are cropped, the fafter the roots increafe ; and,
what is ftill more wonderful is, that the animals
that browfe on graffes, though left at full liberty
in the pafture, leave the ftraws which fupport
the flower and the feed untouched; and what
more clearly manifefts that thefe things are not
the effects of chance, but the refult of Divine
Intelligence, is that thofe fpecies, which flourifh
on the tops of mountains, where the fummer
heats are not fufficient to bring their feeds to
perfection, are generally increafed by the root,
or winter-buds, and do not depend upon the
feed for increafe. Linnæus, according to his
ufual method, has arranged this numerous order
into feveral divifions, marked by their manner
of growth, they are firft divided into thofe that
bear fpikes, and fuch as are produced in pani-
cles ; a panicle is a kind of loofe bunch, in
which

which the flowers grow irregularly, and rather fcattered.   The three firft divifions include thofe that are produced in this manner, and arc diftin-guifhed by the number of flowers in each em-palement.

> The firft divifion has but one flower,
> The fecond two, and
> The third feveral.
> The fourth divifion confifts of all thofe that grow in fpikes or heads.

Befides the plants that fall under this order, there are others of the grafs kind, that differ in fome of their characters, and are referred to their proper claffes and orders.   Vernal Grafs has only two ftamens, and confequently ranks in the clafs Diandria.   We are indebted to this grafs for the delightful fragrance of the new-mown hay.   The various difpofals of the fta-mens and pointals on one plant in Hard Grafs and Soft Grafs, exclude them from this clafs, though, in other refpects, they partake of the ge-neral character.   I have felected the Panic Grafs as an inftance of the firft divifion.   It is known by the following diftinctions : its hufk has three unequal valves, nearly egg-fhaped, the fmalleft of them ftanding behind the other two, contain-ing one floret, which confifts of two valves, not

fo large as thofe of the empalement. The fla-
mens are three; fhort, hair-like, and tipped,
with oblong anthers. The feed-bud is roundifh,
and the two pointals crowned with downy fummits. Each bloffom inclofes a roundifh feed,
flattened a little on one fide. In the next divifion there are but two genera. Hair Grafs and
Rope Grafs, which we will pafs over, as there is
nothing particularly ftriking in their manner of
growth. Quake Grafs, Meadow Grafs, Fefcue,
Broom Grafs, Oat, and Reed, are all pretty
common, and fall under the third divifion. The
genera are diftinguifhed chiefly by the different
form of the corollas, and the fhape of the valves:
there are many fpecies of each genus; but I
muft omit various particulars worthy of your
notice, as my letter is already of an immoderate
length, and I have not yet touched upon the
principal kinds of corn. The effential charaᵬer
of the Oat, confifts in the jointed twifted awn,
or beard, that grows from the back of the bloffom. It is remarkable for the elegance of its
panicle, and the flexibility of the fruit ftalk,
which turns with the flighteft breath of wind.
Among the Reeds, the Sugar Plant is included,
as well as the Bamboo, which grows in the Eaft
Indies. It is time to haften to the fourth and
laft clafs, which contains the individuals of this
family, that are moft important to man, as Rye,

3   Barley,

Barley, Wheat, Darnel, and Dogftail. Thefe are diftinguifhed from the former divifions, by always growing in a fpike or ear.

Rye has two flowers, included in the fame empalement.
Wheat has three.
Barley has a fix-leafed involucre, containing three fimple flowers.
The other two are contained in the involucre of a fingle leaf, and their flowers are compound.

In Rye, there frequently is a third floret upon a fruit-ftalk, between the two larger ones, which have no ftalk. In fome fpecies of Barley, all the three florets, which grow together, have both ftamens and pointals; but, in others, the middle florets alone are furnifhed with thofe parts, the lateral florets having only two ftamens. The exterior valve of the corolla in Wheat is fometimes bearded, but not always. The calyx moftly contains three or four flowers, and the middle one is often imperfect. The filaments in Rye and Wheat are long, and hang out beyond the corolla, which expofes thefe grains to more injury from heavy rains, than that of Barley, in which the filaments are fhorter. Corn is the produce of cultivation, in all countries where it grows; and, what is extraordinary

is, .

is, that it is not known of what country it was originally a native. It differs in excellence, according to the foil and temperature. Wheat prefers a country that is rather warm, and flouriſhes moſt in the ſouthern parts of the temperate zone, rejecting both extremes of heat and cold. This letter will ſupply you with employment till the hay ſeaſon is over. Adieu! Ever yours,

FELICIA.

LETTER X.

DEAR CONSTANCE,   *Shrubbery, May* 3.

THOUGH the graſſes are ſo numerous, and form ſo large a part of the third claſs, they do not exclude others from it, that are worth notice, either on account of their beauty, or peculiarity of conſtruction. The majeſtic tribe of Flag flowers, and the modeſt Crocus, the welcome harbinger of ſpring, with ſome others, belong to it. They are characteriſed by a ſpathe or ſheath, inſtead of an empalement. The corolla either
                                         conſiſts

confifts of fix petals, or is divided fo deeply, as
to appear as if it were fo. The petals of the
different fpecies of Iris have a peculiar conftruction, which claims your notice; the three outward ones are reflected or turned back, the
other three ftand upright, and are fharper;
though they appear as if they were feparated,
they are all connected together by the claws.
In the centre of the flower, there feems to be
three other petals, which in reality are nothing
but the pointal, divided into three parts : it has
a very fhort fhaft, but the ftigma is large, broad,
and reflected; underneath each divifion lies
concealed a fingle flamen, terminated by its
ftraight, oblong, flattened anther. Some of the
fpecies are adorned by a kind of fringed beard
along the middle of the reflex petals, but this
is not common to them all. The capfule is
beneath the flower, and agrees, in its form and
divifions, with the number of the ftigmas, being
triangular; though there are fome kinds that
have fix angles and only three cells. The leaves
of thefe plants are long and narrow, refembling
thofe of grafs, and moftly proceed from the
root. There is an affinity between thefe plants
and the filiaceous tribe, notwithftanding they
are diftinguifhed by fome particulars that place
them in different claffes.

The

The flowers of the next clafs, Tetrandria, are
chara&ifed by having four ftamens ; fo are thofe
of the fourteenth : but it is neceffary to remark,
that thofe, under prefent obfervation, are all of
the fame length, whilft thofe of the fourteenth
are known by their inequality, two of them
being long, and two of them fhort, which is a
diftin&ion that muft never be forgotten. The
firft order is thrown into five divifions ; fome of
the flowers, of which it is compofed, are called
aggregate. At the firft view, you might be
ready to decide that they were compound
flowers ; but, upon a more accurate infpe&ion,
you will find, that befides the florets growing on
one common bafe or receptacle, inclofed by a general cup or empalement, that each little floret has
a feparate cup peculiar to itfelf; thus we may confider them, with more propriety, as a head of dif-
tin& flowers, growing together, than as one compound flower compofed of many parts. Let us
take the Teafel * for an example. The common cup, containing the whole, confifts of many
leaves, which are flexible, and longer than the
florets themfelves ; the receptacle is of a conical
form. The proper cup, belonging to each floret,
is fo fmall as to be fcarcely perceptible ; thofe
of the Scabious †, another genus of this order,
are double. Each individual flower is formed of

* Dipfacus.   † Scabiofa.

one

one tubular-fhaped petal, and they are feparated
from each other by chaffy leaves growing between them. In the fecond divifion, you will
meet with the plantains *, of which there are
feveral fpecies; it is a plant familiarly known to
you, as you frequently gather it for your favourite Goldfinch; but as it is not very beautiful,
perhaps you never examined it minutely. Gather
a head or fpike of it, and you will perceive that
it is compofed of many fmall flowers, which you
muft confider one at a time, to become acquainted with the parts of the fructification. Each of
them has the calyx and the corolla divided into
four fegments, and the border of the latter turned back, as if broken; the filaments are very
long, and the feed-veffel egg-fhaped, with two
cells. In the grafs-leafed Plantain, the ftamens
and pointals are in feparate flowers. The
fourth divifion contains a natural order, called
the Starry Plants, which nearly agree in the following character : they have a fmall cup divided
into four fharp fegments, above the feed-veffel.
The bloffom is monopetalous and tubular, with
an expanding border with four divifions. The
ftamens are four, with fimple tips; the feed-bud
double, containing two globular feeds; the ftigma cloven or divided; and the ftems four cornered, furrounded by the leaves in the form of

* Plantago
D 5   a ftar.

a ftar. Madder *, Goofegrafs †, Woodroof, and
Reedwort are of this family. There is a very
fingular plant belonging to the fecond order,
which I cannot pafs by, without mentioning its
peculiar properties. It is called Dodder ‡, and
is one of that kind that Linnæus has named pa-
rafitical, from the habit of clinging and fupporting themfelves by any other plant that grows
near them. Hops, Flax, and Nettles are its fa-
vourites. It decays at the root, and receives its future nourifhment from the plant to which it adheres, as foon as the young fhoots have twifted
themfelves round the branches of a neighbouring
plant ; they infert a kind of gland into the pores
of its bark, and, by this means extract its juices,
and thus, in return for the fupport and affiftance
they receive, they deftroy their benefactor ; an
inftance, that le ons of morality may be learned
from the vegetable, as well as the animal kingdom. Thofe that entertain flatterers in either,
are generally repaid with ingratitude. With full
affurance that our affection is mutual, and our
gratitude reciprocal, I fubfcribe myfelf entirely
yours,

FELICIA.

* Rubria,   † Galium.   ‡ Cufcula.

LETTER

LETTER. XI.

Shrubbery, May 20.

SO numerous are the objects that the clafs
Pentandria prefents, that I feel myfelf at a lofs
how to felect a few of them for your obfervation. Happily for me, there are feveral natural
orders in this clafs, which, by grouping many of
them together, will enable me to perform my
tafk more eafily. The firft divifion of the firft
order includes a family of plants, whofe leaves
are rough and hairy, and without leaf-ftalks.
Befides this peculiarity, they agree in having a
cup of one leaf, with five clefts or divifions, a
bloffom of a tubular fhape, alfo monopetalous,
and the fame number of fegments; the five ftamens are fixed to the tube of the bloffom, and
they have four naked feeds inclofed by the cup.
Lungwort* is of this order: one fpecies of it
has a rough ftem as well as leaves; the tube is
white, but the border of the bloffom is purple
when it firft opens, but afterwards becomes blue.
You have probably admired the flowers of the
Borrage†, when ufed for the cool tankard in fummer, without remarking that the bloffom is

* Pulmonaria.   † Anchufa.

D 6   wheel-

wheel-fhaped, and the mouth crowned with five
fmall protuberances; the fine blue colour of the
petals, contrafted with the black lips, render it
extremely pleafing to the eye.   Moufe Oar, or
Scorpion Grafs, is common in dry paftures, and
by the fides of rivers.   In fome fpecies of it,
the feeds are covered with hooked prickles,
which, by adhering to whatever touches them, is
a curious method of conveying them from place
to place.   The beauty of the bloffom of this
minute flower repays the pains of examining it
clofely; it is of a celeftial blue, adorned with a
yellow eye.   The generic charafter of Buglofs
confifts in the bending curve of the tube of the
bloffom.   Houndftongue * is diftinguifhed by
each feed being inclofed in four feed-coats,
fixed to the fhaft of the pointal; it has a ftrong
fmell like that of mice, and grows by hedges
and pathways.   The natural order, called Precia,
is included in the fecond divifion of the firft order of this clafs, and receives its name on account of the early appearance of the plants that
compofe it..   The Primrofe*, Oxlip, and Cowf-
lip, the ornament of our meadows, in the early
part of fpring, belong to it.   The Polyanthus
and Auricula, admired and cultivated by florifts,
for their variety and beauty, are derived from
this ftock; a pleafing inftance of the improve-

* Cynogloffum.   † Primula.

ment

ment that art is capable of beſtowing on nature ;
and reſembling, in ſome degree, the difference
between the untutored mind, and that of a per-
ſon of education. The calyx of theſe flowers is
of one leaf, tubular, ſharp, and upright; the
bloſſom alſo tubular, and of one petal, with the
border divided into five ſegments; the ſeed-
veſſel is a capſule, ſuperior, or incloſed within
the calyx, containing only one cell; the ſtigma
is globoſe. The ſpecies is marked by a five angled calyx, the wrinkled ſurface and indented
edges of its leaves. The Primroſe has but one
flower upon a fruit-ſtalk ; the Oxlip and Cow-
ſlip ſeveral. I need not tell you, that the bloſſoms of all theſe are generally of a pale yellow.
The ſame diviſion, of the firſt order of this claſs,
contains a tribe of plants, called Luridæ, a
name expreſſive of their noxious appearance and
ſtrong ſcent, marks kindly impreſſed by nature,
to warn the incautious againſt their baneful effects, moſt of them being poiſonous in a wild
ſtate ; but change of ſoil and cultivation have
rendered even ſome of theſe eatable : others
yield to the ſkill of the phyſician, and, under
proper management, are uſeful in medicine.
Beſides the characteriſtic marks of five ſtamens
and one pointal, they coincide in a calyx, that
is permanent, and divided, like the corolla,
which conſiſts of one petal, into five ſegments.
                                        Their

Their feed-veffel has two divifions, and is either a capfule or a berry, inclofed within the
flower.

A few individuals of this noxious family will
fuffice to guard you againft approaching the reft
too familiarly. The Thornapple* has an oblong
cup of one leaf, divided into five angles and
five teeth, which, though it falls off when the
feeds ripen, leaves part of the bafe behind. The
corolla is funnel-fhaped, fpreading wide from a
long tube into a border, with five angles and
five plaits; in one of the varieties, the bloffom
is white, and, at night, the leaves rife up and
inclofe the flower. The capfule is large and
covered with thorns; it has four divifions, and
grows upright upon the remains of the cup; the
feeds it contains are numerous and kidney fhaped. The fmell of the Henbane†, though very
difagreeable, has not always been fufficient to
deter ignorant perfons from fuffering the fatal
confequences of its poifonous qualities. Mad-
nefs, convulfions, and death, have been produced by it. The common fort is diftinguifhed by
its indented leaves, embracing the ftem, on
which the flowers fit clofe. It has a funnel-
fhaped bloffom, with five blunt fegments, one
broader than the reft. The whole is hairy, and
covered with fœtid clammy juice, defigned,

* Datura.   † Ayafcyamus.

perhaps

perhaps, to drive away infeĉts, which would otherwife be injurious to it. The Nightſhade* is a principal genus in this forbidding order. The wheel-ſhaped corolla, ſhort tube, and large border, ſtamens having oblong lips, approaching ſo nearly as to appear like one objeĉt, in the middle of the bloſſom, with the round gloſſy berry of this tribe, readily diſtinguiſh the plants that belong to it.   Prickly ſtalks charaĉterife ſome of the ſpecies, but others are void of thefe defenſive weapons.   The berry of the woody Nightſhade is red, and its blue bloſſoms ſometimes change to fleſh-colour or white, whilſt the garden Nightſhade is known by its black berries and white bloſſoms.   The Dwale, or deadly Nightſhade, is the moſt fatal in its effeĉts.   The leaves are egg-ſhaped and undivided, the bloſ-ſoms a dingy purple.   Woods, hedges, and gloomy lanes moſtly conceal this dangerous plant; though it too frequently lurks near the huſbandman's cottage, whofe children are endangered by the tempting appearance of its bright ſhining black berries.   The clafs Pentandria compriſes ſo many orders, moſt of which contain genera worthy your attention, that it will ſupply matter for ſeveral letters.   The prefent one being already of ſufficient length, I will

* Solanum.

clofe

close it, with the account of the Luridæ, from whose poisonous influence, I hope you will always be preserved. Farewell.

FELICIA

LETTER XII.

DEAR CONSTANCE,   *Shrubbery, May* 10.

AS I told you at the conclusion of my last letter, that we had by no means exhausted the stores of the fifth class, I shall proceed to give you an account of another family of plants, contained in the first numerous order. A permanent calyx with five divisions, a bell-shaped corolla of one petal, and a capsule for a seed-vessel, are the marks by which the natural order Campanacei, or Bell flowers is known. The elegant genus, Convolvolus, belongs to it, which receives its name from its propensity to entwine itself around any thing near which it grows, though there are some species of it that do not possess this quality. You will easily distinguish the flowers of this kind from all others, by their
large

large, expanding, plaited corolla, flightly indented
at the edge with five or ten notches, the pointal
terminating in two oblong fummits, and the
capfule, containing two roundifh feeds, inclofed
by the cup. The fmall Bindweed * is common
in corn fields, the leaves are arrow-fhaped, fharp
at each angle, the flowers grow fingle upon à
fruit-ftalk, the colour of the bloffom varies, it
is fometimes reddifh, or white, or ftriped, or
purple. This humble trailing plant, though
troublefome to the farmer, poffeffes more beauty
than many that are cultivated for their rarity.
The great Bindweed, another fpecies of the fame
genus, with pure white bloffoms, fo often feen in
fantaftic wreaths, entwined on hedges or bufhes,
is another fpecies. The leaves of this plant are
alfo arrow-fhaped, but the angles at the bafe appear as if they had been cut off, the fruit-ftalk
is four cornered, and fupports a fingle flower;
clofe to the cup are two heart-fhaped floral
leaves, which feem to inclofe it. The Bell
flowers have a honey-cup in the bottom of the
bloffoms, which is clofed at the bafe with five
fharp valves, approaching and covering the receptacle; from thefe valves arife the ftamens;
the ftigma has three divifions, which are turned
backwards. The feed-veffel is a capfule, below
the flower, with three or five cells, at the top

* Convolvolus,

of each is a hole, for the purpofe of letting out the
feeds as foon as they are ripe. What curious provifion is made, not only to preferve the feeds of
plants, but alfo to diftribute them, that the fpecies may not become extinct from negligence or
inattention. The feed-veffels of the Giant
Throatwort*, after the flowers are faded, turn
downwards till they difcharged their contents,
and then rife up again. This plant is known by
its ftrong, round, fingle ftalks, its leaves between
egg and fpear-fhaped, their edges toothed, the
flowers are folitary, growing on nodding fruit-
ftalks, towards the upper part of the ftalk. The
whole plant abounds with a milky liquor. Our
favourite fhrub, the Honeyfuckle †, is included
in the fame order of the fifth clafs, that has engaged fo much of our time. You are well acquainted with its beauty and fragrance, but probably have never minutely examined its parts.
The corolla is monopetalous and irregular, the
tube long, five fegments divide the border,
which are rolled backwards, and one of them is
fcolloped deeper than the others. The feed-
veffel is a berry with two cells placed beneath
the flower, and crowned with the cup. Several
other well-known fhrubs rank in the fame order, fome armed with thorns or prickles, and
others defencelefs; amongft the former is the

Campanula.   † Tonicera.

Buck-

Buckthorn*, from which fap-green is made, by mixing alum with the juice of its ripe berries. The flowers are always incomplete, fome plants producing only thofe that have ftamens, others bearing thofe with a pointal alone. Every part of this fhrub contains the property of ftaining or colouring. In one fpecies, the inner bark is yellow, the outer fea-green, and the middle bark as red as blood. It is ufed by the dyers. Before I difmifs the fhrubs of this order, I muft notice the Currant†, the fruit of which is fo refrefhing and agreeable, whether eaten frefh from the tree, or preferved with fugar. It is found wild in many parts of England. The Periwincle ‡ will fupply me with an example of one more natural order, named Contorta, becaufe the divifions of the corolla are turned in the fame direction with the apparent motion of the fun. There are feveral varieties of it, chiefly diftinguifhed by the different colours of the corolla, which is falver-fhaped, the fegments connected with the top of the tube, which forms a figure of five fides. The general characters of this order are a cup of one leaf, divided into five fegments; a corolla of one petal, frequently funnel-fhaped, and furnifhed with a remarkable nectary, and a fruit, confifting of two veffels, filled with many feeds. I fhall now

* Rhamnus.　† Graffularia.　‡ Vinca.

proceed

proceed to the fecond order of the fifth clafs,
which contains a numerous family, in its third
divifion, of umbelliferous plants, or plants, the
flowers of which are difpofed in rundles; but as
the defcription of them will much exceed the
limits of this letter, I fhall defer them till my
next, and point out a few examples of a different appearance, that belong to this order. The
Grofefoots* are a tribe that will not invite notice by their beauty, being generally deftitute of
bloffom; they are known by a five-leaved, five-
angled, permanent calyx, inclofing one fingle,
round, comprefled feed, when that is ripe, the
calyx falls off, being no longer neceffary. One
fpecies, called Allgood, is fometimes fubftituted
for Spinach. The fame clafs and order includes alfo the Gentians†, which are diftinguifhed from their companions, by an oblong
tapering capfule, flightly cloven at the end; it
has one cell and two valves, to each of which
adheres a receptacle growing lengthwife. The
flowers vary in different fpecies, but the figure
of the fruit is uniform, therefore a proper characteriftic for the botanift, whofe fkill confifts in
difcovering thofe parts, which are conftantly
alike, in all the fpecies of the fame genus.
Linnæus was the firft who perceived the advantage of finding invariable marks, for claffing

* Chenopodium.   † Gentiana.

and.

and arranging the innumerable productions of the vegetable kingdom. Perhaps you will be furprifed to hear, that the ftately Elm * ranks with plants of fuch inferior fize and appearance ; but you muft remember, that it is not the outward form, but the fimilarity of the parts that are invariable, that unites different plants in the fame clafs. Few perfons, but thofe of nice obfervation, know that this tree bears any flower, becaufe it is fmall, and appears in a feafon, when the fire-fide is more inviting to the indolent, than the wholefome walk. The flowers precede the leaves, and foon fall off; the calyx has five clefts, and is coloured on the infide ; it has no corolla, but the feed-veffel is an oval berry without pulp, containing only one feed, rather globular and a little compreffed. The bark of the trunk is crooked and wrinkled, and is ufed as a medicine in feveral diforders. The evening is beautiful, and I am fummoned by Mrs. Snelgrove to attend her in the garden. Love me as well as when we were together, and believe that my attachment is undiminifhed.

FELICIA.

* Ulmus.

LETTER

LETTER XIII.

Shrubbery, May 19.

THE umbellate plants, my dear fifter, are fo termed from their peculiar manner of growth, which differs materially from moft others. From a ftraight ftem, generally hollow and pithy, furnifhed with alternate leaves, proceed fmaller ftems, forming a fharp angle at their bafe, and diverging, or fpreading like rays from a centre, in form of the ribs of an umbrella, which gives them the name of umbellate, each of the ftems, which form thefe rundles or umbels, as they are called, are frequently crowned with a rundlet, or fmaller fet of rays, terminated by the flowers, the parts of which I fhall defcribe more minutely hereafter; as their diftinctions are the principal thing to be obferved, in determining to which clafs or order they belong. The bafe of each circle of ftems is fometimes furrounded with fmall leaves, called an involucre or fence, which is termed general, when it inclofes the whole rundle; and partial, if found at the bafe of the rundlet: many kinds have no fence: thefe differences throw the tribe into three divifions. The firft including the plants with general

fences,

fences, the next thofe with partial ones, and the laft thofe deftitute of any. The properties of this tribe are affected by foil and fituation; thofe in dry places are aromatic and beneficial to the ftomach; but the produce of watery ones are frequently poifonous. Various parts of many individuals of this race, fupply our tables with a pleafing change of vegetables. We eat the roots of Carrots and Parfneps; the ftalks of Celery and Finochia enrich our fallads; the ftems of Angelica, preferved, make a good fweetmeat; the leaves of Parfley and Fennel add a fine flavour to forcemeats and broths; and thofe of Samphire are ufed as a pickle, whilft the feeds of the Coriander and Carraway not only affift digeftion, but, being encrufted with fugar by the confectioner, are eaten in the form of fugar-plums. When you are acquainted with a few of thefe plants, you will probably think their character and appearance fo peculiar, that you fhall not be liable to confound them with others of a different order; but, my dear Conftance, to fecure yourfelf from fuch a miftake, it will be always neceffary to examine the contents of the flower carefully, as the only fure teft to be relied upon. As there are plants of a different conftruction, that refemble thefe in appearance, at leaft to the eye of a fuperficial obferver, without poffeffing the effential requifites of the umbellate tribe; they confift of a

cup

cup fcarcely difcernible, a corolla that grows
upon the feed-bud, formed of five petals, which
are generally heart-fhaped and bent inwards, five
ftamens, and two pointals, upon a naked fruit
compofed of two feeds growing together. The
bloffom of the Elder refembles them greatly at
firft fight, but, on further examination, you will
be convinced that it has no claim to be ranged
among them. After this general account of the
umbellate tribe, you muft be contented with a
few remarks only, concerning fome of the plants
that compofe it, as I am defirous of exciting
your particular attention to the diftinctions of
the various fpecies, which you fhould beftow on
the real individuals, trufting to no written defcriptions, as many of them have a ftrong like-
nefs, as to external appearance, to thofe which
poffefs very oppofite qualities. Parfley and
Fools Parfley, Garden-Chervil and Hemlock-
Chervil, Creeping Water-Parfnep and Water-
Crefs, have been often miftaken for each other,
and the error has produced very difagreeable effects. The beft feafon for acquiring a knowledge of their differences is when they are in
flower, as the plants are then in the fulleft perfection. The Fools-Parfley is known from the
True, by a fence of three, long, narrow, fharp-
pointed leaflets, hanging down under every partial umbel : whereas the fence, in the Garden-
                                        Parfley

Parſley is found at the baſe of the general, as well as the partial umbel, and conſiſts only of a few ſhort folioles, almoſt as fine as hairs. The rank diſagreeable ſmell of the Fools-Parſley, when the ſtem or leaves are bruiſed, is another guide to direct you in knowing it from the True, which at firſt ſight it ſo much reſembles. Hemlock Chervil * is a wild plant, which, notwithſtanding it grows in dry ſituations, ſuch as banks and the ſides of high roads, is of a poiſonous nature, and it not only belongs to the ſame diviſion, but is of the ſame genus as the Garden Chervil; it is, therefore, very liable to be miſtaken for it. The corolla in both is radiate, and the petals notched at the end, the middle flowers are frequently incomplete, and conſequently produce no ſeed. The fruits are of an oblong ſhape. So far they coincide; but the Garden Chervil has the advantage in height, is of a pleaſing aſpect, and is adorned with light-green leaves, whilſt its reſemblance grows lower, and has hairy leaves of a darker colour. As I have told you, that the Creeping Water-Parſnep + has ſometimes been eaten inſtead of the Water-Creſs, of which you are ſo fond, I will acquaint you with their moſt obvious diſtinctions, leſt you ſhould be deprived of the pleaſure of your breakfaſt, from an apprehenſion of being poiſon-

* Scandix.　　　　+ Sium.

E　　　　　　　　　　ed.

ed. They cannot be confounded when in bloffom, the Water Crefs belonging to the cruciform
tribe, but as that is not the time for gathering
this plant, we muſt look for the difference in
their foliage. The winged leaf of the Water-
Parſnep is formed of leaflets longer and narrower than thoſe of the Water-Crefs, with
edges like the teeth of a ſaw, and terminating in
a ſharp point; but if you remark the leaves of
the latter, you will find that they have a browniſh tinge, that the leaflets are of a roundiſh ſhape,
and particularly the one at the end of the winged
leaf, and that the edges are ſmooth, except a few
indentures or curvings. Leaving the umbellate kinds to your future infpeĉion, I ſhall proceed to notice ſeveral trees and ſhrubs which
belong to the third order of the fifth clafs. The
bloſſom of the Meal* Tree has a very ſmall cup,
ſuperior to the ſeed-veſſel, with five teeth; one
bell-ſhaped petal, with five hollow clefts turned
back, its fruit a roundiſh berry of one cell, concealing a ſingle ſeed as hard as bone. The
Guelder Rofe, ſo ornamental to ſhrubberies, with
its ſnow-white flowers, growing in balls, is a variety of the Meal Tree. The Elder†, which I have
warned you to diſtinguiſh from the plants of the
umbellate tribe, is of this order; its beautiful
bloſſoms, nodding like feathers, will afford you

* Vibumum.   † Sambucus.

a ſpeci-

a fpecimen of flowers growing in a cyme.
There is a kind of Elder with variegated leaves,
which have a pretty effect amongft other Shrubs.
Many parts of the Elder are ufeful. Wine is
made both from the flowers and the berries, and
the root is applied as a medicine. The fourth
order contains but two genera, of which the
Parnaffus * is one. This grows wild, but not
very commonly, in marfhy places, the leaves that
are near the root are heart-fhaped on long ftalks,
the ftem-leaves fitting clofe to the ftem. The
feed-bud is open at the top, whilft the plant is
in flower, being deftitute of either fhaft or fummit, the ftamens turn their lips towards the hole,
and fcatter the duft of their anthers into it, which
renders the feeds fertile, and then return to their
former fituation. The petals are white, ftreaked
with yellow, and the honey-cups are remarkable
for their beauty, as well as fingularity. There
are five of them, each hollow and fhaped like a
heart, furrounded with thirteen little fhafts or
pillars, fet along the edge, and each crowned
with a little globe. Thrift †, that pretty pink
flower which edges the borders in the kitchen
garden, is of the fifth order, having five fhafts
with fharp fummits, and five awl-fhaped ftamens
fixed to the claws of the petals : there are twenty-
two fpecies, in which the cup varies as to fhape,

* Parnaffia, † Statice.

E 2 but

but it is always of one leaf, dry and ſhrivelled
like chaff, its corolla is of five petals, narrow at
the baſe but expanded toward the top, and the
flowers growing in a round head upon a ſingle
ſtalk. Before I diſmiſs this numerous claſs, I
muſt preſent you with a plant celebrated for its
extenſive utility. Flax * is of Egyptian origin,
but has long been naturalized in this part of the
world. This ſimple vegetable, of no greater
height than twenty inches, is the chief material
of the linen manufaᵭure, the fibres of the ſtem,
after undergoing various operations, being ſpun
into thread, which is afterwards woven into cloth
of different qualities ; this ſubſtance, when worn
out, is converted into paper, by means of mills
which grind the rags to a pulp. The ſeeds ſupply birds with food, and yield an oil by preſſure
only, that is excellent in diſorders of the lungs ;
painters and varniſhers are indebted to the oil
obtained from Flax Seed ; and the cakes, made
of the huſks, after the oil is ſqueezed out, are
extenſively uſeful to fatten cattle ; the very duſt
is of value, being found an excellent manure.
Were I to enumerate all the purpoſes to which
this plant is applied, it would fill a volume,
rather than a letter, and lead me far away from
the objeᵭ before us, which reminds me to in-
form you, that Flax has a five-leaved calyx, and

* Linum.

a corolla

a corolla of five petals; the capfule opens by five valves, being divided in the infide, into ten cells, each containing one feed. The bloffoms are blue, which are produced on an unbranched ftalk, with alternate lance-fhaped leaves. Having felected a fufficient number of fpecimens of the clafs Pentandria, J fhall clofe my letter, believing that the objects already defcribed will furnifh you with fufficient employment, till I have leifure to collect farther information, relative to thofe that are to follow. This fine feafon fhould encourage you to fpend a great deal of time abroad. Remember to ufe your eyes, and let none of Flora's beauties efcape your obfervation. Adieu.

FELICIA.

LETTER XIV.

DEAR CONSTANCE, *Shrubbery, June 1.*

THE clafs Hexandria, or flowers with fix ftamens, includes the far greater part of the liliaceous tribe, but do not fuppofe that it confifts of them alone, other plants are to be found in it,

E 3 though

though comparatively few in number. Our gardens receive many of their moft fplendid embellifhments from the flowers of this defcription. The gaudy Tulip, with its ftriped coral of varied hues, produced by the art of the florift from a fingle colour in its natural ftate, has been fo highly rated for its beauties by Dutch con- noiffeurs, as to be fold for one hundred ducats the fingle root. The Hyacinth of different co- lours, and delightful fragrance, the whole family of Lilies, the magnificent Amaryllis, the great American Aloe, that rifes to the height of twen- ty feet, with all the leffer plants of that denomi- nation, rank among thofe of the liliaceous kind, with many more remarkable for the delicacy of their form, and the fplendor of their colours; but as moft of thefe are of foreign extraction, I fhall pafs them over as objects of admiration only, and fearch among the humble plants of our own growth for a few, worthy of minute defcription; fome of this family have a calyx, others are entirely without, and the buds of many of them are inclofed in a fheath or hufk, which burfts as the coral expands: this circum- ftance throws them naturally into three fubdivi- fions. Among the plants of the latter, is the elegant Snowdrop*, fo much valued by thofe who delight in the return of fpring, as one of its

* Galanthus.

carlieft

earlieft harbingers. Its corolla is fuperior, and confifts of fix white petals, a little tinged with green, of which the three innermoft are the fhorteft, and are fuppofed to be the nectary. This beautiful little flower never appears to more advantage, than when it intermixes its, bloffoms with thofe of the Golden Crocus, which is nearly related to the fame tribe, by its manner of growth and external ftructure; the calyx. is a fheath, and the corolla has fix divifions, the tube defcending towards the root; but it is feparated from it, by the artificial fyftem, as it has only three ftamens and one pointal.. Meadow Saffron *, which is very like the Crocus, however belongs to it, and is included in the third order of this clafs. It is found in the month of September in paftures, with flat fpear-fhaped leaves, and pale purple bloffoms, which are doubled by cultivation, and changed into various colours. But to return to the firft order, from whence I have wandered a little, for the fake of uniting the Crocus with the Snowdrop. The Daffodil and the Narciffus have only one flower, produced from the fame fheath; their general characters confift of fix petals, forming a fuperior corolla, a funnel-fhaped honey-cup of one leaf, containing the ftamens which are fixed to its tube. The Hyacinths, cultivated with fo

* Colchicum,

E 4   much

much care, are frequently double, and the bloſ-
foms are of various colours; but whatever pleafure they yield us, as objects of fight and ſmell,
we muſt reject them for the wild Harebell, in
which we ſhall be able to trace their original
features, unimproved by the poliſhing hand of
art. The Hyacinth in its native ſtate has no
empalement, its bloſſom is bell-ſhaped, and of
one petal, the border divided into ſix clefts, and
turned back; at the point of the feed-bud are
three pores filled with honey. The modeſt Lily
of the Valley* differs from the Harebell, in its
feed-veſſel, which is a round berry, ſpotted before it is ripe, whilſt that of the Harebell is a
capſule. Solomon's Seal is diſtinguiſhed from
the Lily of the Valley, by its ſtem being clothed
with alternate leaves, whereas the Harebell has
a naked ſtalk. The Barberry is a ſhrub that
belongs to this firſt order of the ſixth claſs,
though it has no pretenſions to range with the
liliaceous tribe, its leaves change into thorns.
A fine ſweetmeat is made of its berries, the ears
of corn that grow in its neighbourhood never
fill, its baneful influence in this refpect extends
ſome hundred yards. The ſtamina are extremely
irritable, if the threads are touched ever ſo ſlightly, the tips approach the pointal, and ſcatter the
pollen with expanſive force. All the ſpecies of

* Convallaria.

Ruſh

Rufh and fome others, which are deficient in the corolla, belong to the fame order. Rice is almoft the only plant known in the fecond order of this clafs, and is chiefly produced in the Eaft and Weft Indies. The Docks* are a numerous genus, belonging to the third order; their beauty is not attractive, they are known by a cup of three leaves, a corolla of three petals, not unlike the cup, but larger; they have no feed-veffel, but the petals, bending in a three cornered form, inclofe the feed, which is triangular. The fifth order contains the Water Plantains †, which are diftinguifhed by a cup of three leaves, a corolla of three large, flat, circular petals, greatly expanded, fucceeded by more than five capfules, each concealing one feed. They are found in ditches and other fhallow waters. The feventh is the fmalleft of all the claffes: I fhall prefent you with but one fpecimen of it. The cup of the Winter green, or Chickweed, has feven fpear-fhaped leaves, the bloffom is formed like a ftar, and, though divided into feven fegments, is of one petal. It has a globular feed-veffel, which is a berry not unlike a capfule, of one cell, with a very thin coat, opening by feveral feams. Although feven is the general number found on this plant, it fometimes deviates from it. In one fpecies of it, the parts of the fructification are

* Rumex.   † Alifma.

E 5   defended

defended againſt the injuries of rain, by the
cloſing of the petals, and hanging down of the
flowers at its approach. In the eighth claſs are
found the Willowherbs*, geneɪally charaɛteriſ-
ed by a ſuperior cup of four tapering coloured
leaves, a corolla of four circular expanding
petals, the ſummit of the pointal divided into
four clefts, a very long capſule of four cells,
containing numerous ſeeds crowned with a feather, doubtlefs to waft them to a diſtance, when
mature. In ſome ſpecies the ſtamens and pointals are upright, but lean towards the lower ſide
of the bloſſom in others. The ſhape of the
leaves is another diſtinɛtion that marks the different ſpecies, as well as their manner of growth;
the ſmall-flowered hairy Willowherb has ſpear-
ſhaped, woolly, toothed leaves, growing oppoſite to one another. The great flowered Willowherb, vulgarly called Codlings and Cream,
has its leaves running along, and embracing the
ſtem; the top ſhoots have a very delicate ſmell,
but it is loſt almoſt as ſoon as they are gathered.
Theſe plants are generally found in marſhy
places, or on the banks of rivers. Heaths and
commons, eſpecially in the northern counties of
England, produce the Whortle†. The moor-
game live upon the berries in autumn; ſome
kinds of them are alſo eaten freely by the com-

* Epilobium.   † Vaccinium.

mon people; they make pleafant tarts or jelly,
and are flavoured much like the American Cran-
berry. They are generally known by a very
fmall cup, a bloffom of one petal, bell-fhaped,
with four clefts rolled backwards. The feed-
veffel is a roundifh berry with a hollow dimple,
divided into four cells, in which are found a few
fmall feeds. Some fpecies are evergreen, others
lofe their leaves at the approach of winter, which
naturally throws them into two divifions. The
Black-worts, or Wind-berry, and the Great Bilberry Bufh belong to the latter; their fruit ftalks
fupport a fingle flower, but the leaves of the
Black-worts are toothed like a faw, and the
bloffom divided into five clefts, whilft the Great
Bilberry Bufh has oval leaves with fmooth
edges. Numerous fpecies are contained in the
Heath* genus, the beauty of the foreign forts
has introduced them into our greenhoufes,
where they do not fhrink from a comparifon
with the brilliant productions of diftant countries collected together. Many of our own
would be valued as beautiful, were they lefs
common, but fuch is our perverfenefs, that whatever is difficult to be obtained, we efteem in proportion to that difficulty. They moftly agree in
thefe characters—a calyx of four leaves, upright,
coloured, inclofing the germ, a bloffom of one

* Erica.

E 6   petal,

petal, cut into four fegments, the figure of which
varies between egg-fhaped and oblong, the
threads of the ftamens ftanding on the receptacle, tips cloven at the point, and a capfule
of four cells. The ftamens in fome fpecies are
longer, and in others fhorter than the bloffom.
Common Heath has the tips inclofed within the
bloffom, which is bell fhaped; its leaves are oppofite and arrow-fhaped. In our happy climate,
this plant is but little regarded, except for its
honey, with which it fupplies the bees in abundance. It is only ufed for inferior purpofes,
fuch as making befoms and firing for ovens;
but in the barren highlands of Scotland it is of
extenfive ufe; the poor cottagers make the walls
of their wretched cabins of alternate layers of
Heath, and a kind of mortar made of black
earth mixed with ftraw, and the roofs are thatch-
ed with it. So deftitute of domeftic comforts
are thefe poor people, that they are contented
with beds formed of the fame material; they con-
trive to make them foft enough to fleep upon, by
placing the roots downwards, and the tops only
appearing at the furface. Mrs. Snelgrove tells
me, that as we advance in the fcience of botany,
we muft not confine our information to the
form of plants, or the number of their parts, but
fhould extend our refearches to the purpofes to
which they are applied; a ftudy that will fupply

3   us

us with much ufeful knowledge and entertainment at the fame time. The ftalks of the crofs-
leafed Heath are fhrubby, and rife from nine to
twelve inches high ; the leaves are fringed with
hairs, and grow in fours, like a crofs, preffed
clofe to the ftalk, each of the hairs at the edge
of the leaves appears, in a magnifying glafs, to
terminate in a fmall round globule. The corolla is nearly oval, of a pale red colour, forming a
little head, one flower hanging down over another. The tips are inclofed in the bloffom.
The Mezereon* is included in the fame order
with thofe already mentioned, in the clafs Octandria, the early bloffoms of which adorn our
fhrubberies in February. It has no cup, but a
funnel-fhaped corolla of one petal, inclofing the
ftamens, and the border cut into four fegments.
The fruit is a berry, in which is found a fingle
feed. The fort commonly cultivated, is diftinguifhed by its flowers growing by threes, from
the fame joint, fitting upon the ftem. The
leaves are fpear-fhaped. The buds at the ends
of the ftalks produce leaves, thofe on the fides
flowers, which are fo thick fet, as to make the
branches appear of a beautiful rofe colour.
There is another fpecies that bears yellowifh
green bloffoms, and is valued as an evergreen.
The third order contains a numerous genus,

* Daphne.

among

among the fpecies of which is the family of Snakeweeds†. They concur in having a turban-fhaped cup, coloured within, and divided into five fegments, which, if you pleafe, you may term the corolla, and then the cup will be wanting. The flowers of the Greater Biftort grow in a fpike on an undivided ftem. The lower leaves are fomewhat heart-fhaped, and continued down the ftalk. The root is one of the moft powerful vegetable aftringents. Knot-Grafs is found commonly by road fides and corn fields. It has a trailing ftem, and the flowers are produced at the bafe of the leaves, which vary much in form, but are generally inclined to fpear-fhaped. The feeds fupply food to great numbers of fmall biids. If my letters are too long, tell me fo, and I will correct my prolixity, or at leaft endeavour to reftrain it within moderate bounds. But when I am writing to my dear Conftance, the time is infenfibly beguiled, and I forget the neceffity of concluding. Moft tenderly your

FELICIA.

* Polygonum.

LETTER

LETTER XV.

DEAR CONSTANCE,   *Shrubbery, June* 6.

THE pleafure I feel in writing to you, is the caufe that I never want leifure for this agreeable employment; if my tafks do not afford me time, I can readily fteal an hour from thofe allotted to fleep or diverfion. I am fully convinced that inclination is always wanting, when one friend cannot find opportunity to write to another. The Flowering Rufh* is the only plant, found wild in England, that belongs to the clafs Enneandria. It grows in the water, and has a round fmooth ftalk, which rifes from one to fix feet high, according to its fituation; at the top of which is a head or umbel of bright red flowers, fometimes not lefs than thirty, furrounded at the bottom of the umbel by an involucre of withered fheaths; three fhort leaves form the cup, the corolla has fix petals. It has fix pointals, and fix long tapering capfules of one valve, opening inwards, filled with numerous fmall feeds. This plant, fo ftately from its height and its beautiful tuft of flowers, would make a charming appearance in canals or other

* Butomus,

pieces

pieces of water, if introduced and cultured by
art : and, as it is fo hardy as to defy the cold of
Lapland, there would be no reafon to fear the
utmoft feverity of froft.   Many remarkable foreign plants belong to this clafs, it will be fufficient to enumerate a few of them.   Bay, Cin-
namon, Caffia, Camphor, and Saffafras, are
comprehended under one genus, and are moft of
them ufeful for medicinal purpofes.   Rhubarb, fo
well known as a ftomachic, is alfo of the fame
clafs, and is fuccefsfully cultivated in this country ; but as its extraction is foreign, it does not
come within my plan to give a further account
of it.   The tenth clafs will fupply us with a
greater variety; Linnæus has conveniently divided the firft order into fuch as have corollas
of many petals, thofe of one petal, and fuch as
are without any.   The firft of thefe are again
divided into fuch as have irregular, and thofe
which have equal corollas.   Birdfneft * has no
empalement, unlefs you give that name to the
five outermoft coloured petals of the corolla,
which are hunched at the bafe, and have a cavity
for honey on the infide ; it has five others, all of
an oblong fhape, upright, and nearly parallel.
The feed-veffel is pentangular, and egg-fhaped,
with five valves containing many chaffy feeds.
Thefe are the characters by which the terminat-

* Monotropa.

ing

ing flower is known; but it is worth your notice to remark, that if there be any lateral flowers, you muſt ſubtraĉt one-fifth of every part of the fruĉtification. This is the caſe with many other plants, which makes it neceſſary to examine the central or principal flower. In ſome plants the ſide flowers have a fifth more of the parts than the primary one. The Strawberry Tree * is a beautiful ſhrub, bearing bunches of white flowers of the preſent year, whilſt the red berries of the laſt ſeaſon remain pendant upon it. It grows without culture in the weſt of Ireland, near the Lake of Killarney, on barren lime-ſtone rocks, and is eſteemed a great ornament to the romantic views of that delightful ſituation. It is known by a very ſmall cup, an egg-ſhaped corolla of one petal, with five ſmall refleĉted ſegments; the ſeed-veſſel is a roundiſh berry, with five cells filled with ſmall ſeeds, as hard as bone. The ſtem is woody, and the leaves ſmooth, but tooth-ed at the edges. In one ſpecies the ſtems trail, and the leaves are wrinkled, with black berries ſitting upon a very ſmall red cup. The ſecond order preſents us with the Saxifrages† a numer-ous genus, of which the pyramidal ſedum is one, which ſtood laſt ſummer on the hall chim-ney-piece, whoſe beautiful cone of white flowers remained ſome weeks in bloſſom. They

* Arbutus.　　　† Saxifraga.

are

are diftinguifhed by a calyx divided into five
parts, a coral of five expanding petals, narrow
towards the bafe, a capfule of one cell, terminating with two beaks, or fharp points, in which
are lodged many minute feeds. The white Sax-
afrage has a beaded root, compofed of a number
of little grains or bulbs, conne&ed together in
clufters by the fibres. The ftem is hairy, a little
branched, and grows about a foot high; the
leaves next the root, placed on long foot-ftalks,
are kidney-fhaped; the flowers terminate the
ftalk in fmall bunches, the coral is white, ftreaked with yellowifh veins. It thrives beft in gra-
velly foils, flowers in May, and produces its
feeds in the month following. The genus Di-
anthus includes the rich Carnation, with its
fpicy odour; the modeft Sweet William, and
the whole tribe of Pinks in all their varities.
Charming as thefe obje&s are rendered in the
garden, by their colours and fragrance, as on
former occafions, we muft have recourfe to the
fields, in fearch of fome of the fpecies that are
to be found there, in a ftate of nature. They
agree in having a cup formed like a cylinder,
toothed at the mouth, and encompaffed at the
bafe with four fcales. A corolla of five petals,
with claws as long as the cup, fixed to the receptacle, and fcolloped at the edges; a cylindric capfule of one cell, opening at the top in
four

four directions. The principal thing to be obferved in afcertaining the fpecies of this beautiful genus, is the manner of flowering. The
Sweet William has its flowers incorporated, or
one head formed of many fingle flowers. Pinks
have feveral flowers proceeding from the fame
ftem, not in bunches, but folitary or feparate.
One fpecies is known by a low herbaceous ftem,
fupporting a fingle flower. The form of the
fcales is another circumftance, which diftinguifhes the fpecies. In the Sweet William they
are as long as the corolla, thofe of the Carnation
and Pink are very fhort. The bloffoms of the
wild Childing Sweet William expand about
eight in the morning, and clofe about one in the
afternoon. What is the caufe of this peculiarity ? Many other plants fhut up their bloffoms at
a particular hour, doubtlefs this inftinct is beftowed on them for fome wife purpofe of prefervation, which is worthy the attention of botanifts to difcover. The Sandworts * and Stitch-
worts are found in the third order, and have a
great fimilitude to each other. They both have
a capfule with one cell, in the former the petals
are of one piece, but in the latter they are divided almoft to the bafe. The genera of Campion † and Catchfly † have alfo a near refemblance, the capfules of both being divided into

* Arenaria.   † Lychnis.

three

three cells, and their petals cloven ; but the
Catchflies are diſtinguiſhed by the honey-cup,
which is compoſed of two little teeth at the
neck of each petal, forming a kind of crown at
the mouth of the tube. All four have five petals in the corolla. Among the plants of the
fourth order are found the Stonecrops*, ſo called
from growing on walls, roofs of houſes, or
rocks, where there appears ſcarcely any mould to
nouriſh them ; one ſpecies, the Sedum Acre,
will flouriſh when hung up by the root, a proof
that it receives its principal ſuſtenance from the
air ; which is the caſe with moſt of the ſucculent
plants. They are generally known by a calyx
cut into five ſegments, a corolla of five petals,
five honey-cups, conſiſting of a ſmall ſcale, placed at the baſe of each germen. Five capſules,
with as many pointals, and twice the number of
ſtamens, the charaċteriſtic marks of the claſs and
order. The different ſpecies of Cuckow-flower,
or Lychnis, agree in having a tubular cup of one
leaf, a corolla compoſed of five petals, frequently cloven, and a capſule with one ceil and five
valves. The names of Meadow Pink, Wild
Williams Ragged Robin, and Cuckow-flowers
are pplied to one ſpecies, which abounds in
moiſt meadows, and is entitled, for its beauty, to
a place in our gardens ; the ſtems are trailing,

* Sedum.

but

but upright, when in flower; the petals are of a fine red, and deeply jagged at the edges. The appearance of the bloſſoms about the time of the cuckow's return, has probably given riſe to its laſt name. In the Campion Cuckow-flower the ſtamens grow upon one plant, and the pointals upon another. The Clammy Cuckow-flower has undivided petals and capſules with five cells. The Woodſorrel * is generally found in woods and moiſt ſhady lanes; and, contrary to expeſtation, the ſame plant thrives on mountains; which is accounted for, by an obſervation of Linnæus, that the clouds, reſting upon the tops of mountains, produce the ſame ſtate of atmoſphere as fogs in low marſhy ſituations. Breakfaſt bell rings, and I muſt obey its call. Farewell.

FELICIA.

LETTER XVI.

DEAR CONSTANCE,   *Shrubbery, June* 10.

A NEW riſen ſun, ſhining into my chamber windows, has awakened me rather earlier than uſual, but I do not repine at being diſturbed, as

* Oxalis.

it

it affords me a convenient opportunity of renewing my fubject. The eleventh clafs, Dodecan-
dria, will prefent us with fome difficulties, but
they may be overcome by patient attention.
The number of ftamens is by no means certain:
all plants, that have from twelve to nineteen
inclufive, belong to it; provided they are fixed
to the receptacle, which is an important circumftance to be obferved, as the number of ftamens
cannot be relied upon. Some plants have lefs
than twelve, and others more than nineteen.
Loofeftrife * has a cylindrical cup of one leaf,
with twelve teeth, inclofing the germ, a corolla
of fix petals, fixed by the claws to the divifions
of the cup. a capfule of two cells, in which are
lodged many fmall feeds. Its purple fpikes
adorn the banks of rivers in July; there is a
variety with a fix-cornered ftem, and the leaves
growing three together; this fpecies has twelve
ftamens, but in fome others there are not fo
many. In the common Agrimony†, the number
of ftamens is equally uncertain: you may find
twelve in fome plants, fometimes ten, and frequently feven. It has a fmall calyx, cut into
five fegments, furrounded by another cup, a corolla of five petals, growing to the cup, and one
or two roundifh feeds in the bottom of the calyx;
the ftem leaves are winged, the odd one at the

* Lythrum.　　　Agrimonia.

end

end fupported upon a leaf-ftalk. The feeds are covered with briftles, and the yellow bloffoms grow in fpikes. The third order confifts of two genera, Yellow-weed * and Spurge †, both very difficult to afcertain, on account of the irregularity of the parts, with refpeĉt to figure and number. The effential charaĉter of the firft is marked by the petals with three clefts, one of them. containing the honey-cup in its bafe, and a capfule of one cell, always open ; the cup is of one leaf, divided into fegments, two of them more gaping than the reft, being diftended by the honey-cup petals. Dyers Weed is found on barren ground, or on walls, and affords a moft beautiful yellow dye for cotton, woollen, filk, or linen ; the yellow hue of the paint, called Dutch Pink, is procured from the ftems and roots of this plant, in which the quality of tinging refides. The ancient Britons are fuppofed to have ftained their bodies with the juice of it. The cup is cut into four fegments, the petals are three, the upper one, bearing the honey-cup, is divided nearly half way into fix parts. The petals that grow on the fides, and oppofite to each other, have only three fegments ; and fometimes two very fmall entire petals grow below them. The flowers blow in a nodding fpike, which follows the courfe of the fun, turning towards

* Refeda.   † Euphorbia.

it,

it, when it rifes, and bending after it, till it finks
beneath the weſtern horizon. At night it points
to the north. A cloudy ſky has not influence
to prevent the faithful attachment of this flower
to the ſun. Spurge has a cup of one leaf, cut
into four (and in ſome) five ſegments, the corolla varies in like manner with reſpect to the
number of its petals, which are in ſome four
and in others five, hunched thick, irregularly
ſituated, and fixed by their claws to the edge of
the cup. The ſtamens are twelve or more, appearing at different periods. The ſeed-veſſel is
a capfule, that is either ſmooth, hairy, or warty,
confiſting of three cavities united, each containing one ſeed, and opening as with a ſpring even
while they are green. The numerous ſpecies
of this genus are conveniently divided into,
thoſe that bear flowers in rundles, with three
diviſions; others that have rundles, with five
diviſions; and thoſe whoſe rundles have many
diviſions. Moſt of the Spurges are filled with a
milky gummy juice, which is very ſharp and cor-
roſive. There is a great reſemblance between
ſome of the plants of this natural family; two
of them, that have a ſtrong ſimilitude to each
other, are frequently cultivated in gardens; but
a cloſe examination will teach us to diſtinguiſh
the one from the other. The leaves of the Sun
Spurge are notched or ſerrated at the edges, but
                                                    in

in the fmall Garden Spurge they are entire.
The petals, or nectaria, of the former, are round
and even at the edges, whilft thofe of the latter
are armed with two little horns. The rundles
of the fmall Garden Spurge have three divifions,
which are feparate in pairs; thofe of the Sun
Spurge have five divifions, with five leaves,
which divide again into three clefts, with three
leaves, and then fork into pairs. The fame
number prevails in every part of the bloffom of
the ·Houfeleek *, the divifions of the cup, the
petals of the corolla, the ftamens, feed-buds,
and capfules, vary from fix to twelve: this genus has a near affinity to the Stonecrop, but
differs from that, in always having more than
five petals. It generally grows-on walls or the
roofs of houfes. Feeling an inclination for exercife, I fhall lay my pen afide till a future occafion. My warmeft affections attend you, and
thofe you are with.

FELICIA.

* Sempervivum.

F   LETTER

LETTER XVII.

DEAR CONSTANCE,   *Shrubbery, June* 15.

THE fatisfaction you kindly exprefs, at my
feeble attempts to amufe you with the refult of
my botanical rambles, encourages me to proceed to the clafs Icofandria, in which the number of the ftamens is not fo much to be confidered, as their fituation. The claffic character,
which diftinguifhes it, both from the clafs laft
defcribed, and that which will fucceed, is, that
the ftamens proceed directly from the fides of
the cup, or united with the bloffom; but not
from the receptacle, as is common in the other
claffes. The petals alfo are fixed to the fides of
the cup by their claws, and the cup confifts of
one leaf, which is not flat, but hollow. The
plants of this clafs form a natural one, the fruits
of which are pulpy and eatable. The Apple *,
Pear *, Cherry, and Plum, being of the number,
I would not have you infer from this, that it is
confined to trees and fhrubs, for there are many
herbs that find a place in it. The Prune, a
genus of the firft order, comprifes the Cherry,
Plum, and Sloe; they agree in the following

* Pyrus.

characters,

characters : a cup of one leaf, bell-shaped with
five clefts, five hollow expanding petals, fixed
to the cup, from twenty to thirty stamens stand-
ing also on the cup ; the feed-veffel is a pulpy
fruit, including a nut or stone which is the feed.
The flowers of the Birds-cherry grow in
bunches, but thofe of the Black-cherry are produced in rundles, on very short fruit-stalks ; the
leaves are gloffy, and doubled together. It is
found in woods and hedges, and abounds particularly in fome parts of Hertfordshire. The
Bullace, from which the cultivated Plums derive their origin, has its fruit-stalks either in
pairs or folitary, and one fpecies has thorny
branches. If you should be induced to gather
the fruit of thofe trees, with the expectation of
enjoying the rich flavour of their congeners in
our orchards, you will be greatly difappointed,
particularly in the wild plums, which are acid
and ungrateful to the tafte ; cultivation beftows
on them fize and fweetnefs ; the art of budding
or grafting them has produced a great many
kinds, diftinguifhed by their peculiar colour,
shape, and flavour. The fecond order contains
but one genus, the Hawthorn * ; the characters
in which the different fpecies concur, are a cup,
divided into five parts, fitting on the top of the
germ, a corolla compofed of five petals, and a

* Cratægus.

F 2   flefhy

flefhy berry containing two feeds. The leaves
of the Whitebean Tree are egg-fhaped, and
jagged, their under furfaces downy. The Wild
Service Tree * has heart-fhaped leaves, with feveral angles. The leaves of the White Thorn
are blunt, with three indentures: it frequently
deviates from the general charaĉter, by having
only one pointal and one feed in each flower.
The principal diftinĉtion, between the fhrubs of
the fecond and third orders, confifts in the number of the pointals. The fourth order, known
by its five pointals, comprehends three genera,
the Medlar †, Apple, (in which Pears are included) and Meadow-fweet. Their common
charaĉters are, a five-toothed cup, and a corolla
of five petals. Their diftinĉtive marks confift
in the diverfity of their fruits : in the firft it is
a berry, in the fecond an apple, and in the third
a fet of capfules. The Rofe ‡, fo univerfally
admired, as the queen of flowers, belongs to the
fifth order ; the different fpecies agree, in a cup
with five divifions, a corolla of five petals, and a
turban-fhaped flefhy berry, formed out of the
cup, and terminated by the divifions of it, inclofing feveral oblong hairy feeds, adhering to
the cup on all fides. Their diftinĉtions chiefly
confift in the form of the fruit, whether inclin-
ing to round or oval, the fituation of the fpines,

* Sorbus.   † Mefpilus.   ‡ Rofa.

on

on the different parts of the fhrub, and the manner of flowering. This general favourite has received all the advantages which art can beftow on it, the varieties are numerous, produced by cultivation ; fcarcely any garden is fo mean as to be deftitute of a Rofe. The Strawberry *, of which fo many kinds are produced by the fkill of the gardener, has the cup divided into ten fegments, but the number of the petals is only five ; the feeds are fcattered upon the furface of the receptacle, commonly called a berry. Having come to the conclufion of this clafs, I fhall likewife clofe my letter ; not that I have exhaufted all the fpecimens it affords, but have defcribed thofe that appear to me to have the beft claim to your notice. Adieu!

FELICIA.

LETTER XVIII.

DEAR CONSTANCE,   *Shrubbery, June 21.*

FREQUENTLY am I tempted abroad, when indolence would keep me within doors, in fearch of fpecimens for my next letter ; thus, many

---

* Fragaria.

F 3   advantages

advantages refult from the purfuit of one objeft.
In the thirteenth clafs, Polyandria, the ftamens are
numerous, fpringing from the receptacle, along
with the pointal ; which is a material diftinction
from thofe that belong to the former clafs, which
I have remarked to be always attached to the cup.
The objects of our prefent confideration are,
many of them, pleafing to the eye, but unlike
thofe delicious and wholefome fruits, lately defcribed ; in their qualities, being poifonous to
the human conftitution. In the firft order is
found the Poppy *, which has a cup of two
leaves, which falls off as the flower expands, a
corolla of four petals, and a capfule of one cell,
crowned with the fummit, and opening beneath
it with many holes ; through thefe the numerous
fmall feeds find a paffage. The feed-veffel in
fome fpecies is round, in others oblong; it is
fmooth in fome kinds, and befet with ftrong
hairs in others ; the number of rays in the fummit is not always the fame. Opium, fo celebrated for its faculty of ftilling the fevereft pain,
is made from the milky juice of the Wild
Poppy. The fame order contains the Water
Lily †, whofe beautiful flowers adorn flow rivers
and ponds in the months of July and Auguft.
The calyx is compofed of four large leaves coloured on the upper furface, the petals of the

Papaver.   † Nymphæ.

corolla

coralla are numerous, frequently as many as fif-
teen; it has a large egg fhaped feed-bud, a circular flat fummit, not fupported by any fhaft, but
fitting, and marked with rays. There are two
fpecies, the flowers of the firft grow on fruit-
ftalks, the bloffoms are yellow. Thofe of the
fecond open about feven in the morning, and
clofe about four in the afternoon, and then lie
on the furface of the water. The fummits are
numerous and placed in a circle, correfponding
in number with the cells in the feed-veffel. The
corollas are a delicate white. As foon as thefe
fplendid water-flowers have perfected their fructification, by the abforption of the pollen by the
pointal, their long ftalks, which always grow in
proportion to the depth of the water, in order to
raife the corollas above it, refufe their fupport,
and the flowers fink down many feet beneath
the furface. There is a remarkable contrivance
exhibited in the procefs of the fructification of the
Vallifenefia of Italy, alfo a water-plant worth
mentioning. The ftamens and pointals are difpofed on different plants, whilft both are in
bloffom; the anthers fall off, and floating among
the piftilliferous flowers, fertilize them with
their pollen. A cup of five leaves, two fmaller
than the reft, a corolla of five petals, and a capfule, covered by the cup, are the characteriftics of
the genus Ciftus, to which many beautiful fhrubs

belong,

belong, though fome of them are herbaceous.
In different kinds, the corollas are either purple,
white, or yellow. The Lime * feldom brings
more than one feed to perfection, and this
pufhes afide the others that are barren, fo that a
carelefs obferver might fuppofe that the capfule
had but one cell, whereas it has five. The
Larkfpur †, belonging to the third order, the Columbine ‡ to the fifth, and the Hellebore § to
the laft, with fome others, unite in having feveral
capfules joined together, no cup, a corolla of
five petals, and a numerous fet of ftamens. The
differences of their honey-cups, which are remarkable, ferve to point out their generic diftinctions; the Larkfpur is known from its companions, by three capfules, and a honey-cup that
is cloven; the front ftanding in the midft of the
petals, and turning backwards like a horn or
fpur. Columbine has five capfules of a cylindrical form, and five equal honey-cups, fhaped
like a cornucopia, fituated alternately between
the petals. Cultivation frequently increafes the
number of thefe nectaries, and diminifhes that of
the petals: when they grow wild, the bloffoms
are blue, but are found of various hues in gardens. Hellebore has feveral capfules, and many
very fhort honey-cups forming a circle round
the outfide of the ftamens; their fhape refem-

* Tilia.   † Delphinium.   ‡ Aquilegia.   § Helleborus.

bles

bles a tube, with the mouth divided into two
lips. After fo many fimilar examples, you will
not be furprifed to hear, that we owe the various-
coloured Anemonies, that adorn the flower-beds
early in fpring, to two fpecies only ; both found
commonly in woods, in the month of April ;
this plant is diftinguifhed from its rival, the Ranunculus, by the want of an empalement, which,
in the latter, confifts of five leaves ; but the effential chara&ter of this genus is marked by the
honey-cup ; in fome fpecies it is a naked pore,
in others it is furrounded by a cylindrical border,
and it is fometimes clofed by a fcale indented at
the end. There are three kinds of Butter-cups,
which are fpecies of the Ranunculus, which give
a golden hue to our meadows by the brilliancy
of their yellow bloffoms, one of them has a bulbous root, fomething like a turnip, the leaves of
the cup bent backward, the fruit-ftalks furrowed, each fupporting a fingle flower. The fecond fort has an open cup, and throws out creeping fuckers ; the laft grows taller than the other
two, its cup is open, and the fruit-ftalk round.
The yellow colour of butter is attributed to the
cows feeding on this plant, but, like many commonly received opinions, it is probably an error,
as it is fo acrimonious, that cattle feldom eat it,
unlefs preffed by hunger. Although my letter is
not fo long as ufual, 1 am inclined to clofe it,

F 5   with

with an account of the specimens of the clafs
Polyandria, thinking I fhall preferve greater per
fpicuity, by confining the fubject of one letter
to the fame clafs. With all fifterly affection I
am yours,

FELICIA.

LETTER XIX.

DEAR CONSTANCE,   *Shrubbery, June 29.*

THE effential character of the fourteenth
clafs, Didynamia, confifts in four ftamens to
each flower, one pair fhorter than the other; the
fhorteft pair grow together, and adhere to the
fhaft of the pointal. The orders are not diftinguifhed, as in the former claffes, by the number
of the pointals, becaufe none of the flowers have
more than one, which, with the ftamens, is inclofed by an irregular corolla of one leaf. The
manner in which the feeds are difpofed, is the circumftance upon which the refpective orders depend. The firft, called Gymnofpermia, has four
naked feeds fixed to the bottom of the cup, without

out any feed-veffel. The other (for there are
but two) denominated Angrofpermia, has the
feeds included in a capfule. The firft order
contains thofe plants that grow in whorls, moft
of them have a fquare ftalk, and their leaves are
produced in pairs. The perfonate flowers are
comprehended in the fecond; but its diftinctive
character refts upon the feeds being contained
in a capfule. The conftruction of thefe flowers,
in general, is curioufly adapted to preferve the
tips of the ftamens from the injuries of the weather, as alfo to convey their duft to the fummit
of the pointal, which is neceffary to render the
feeds fertile. They grow nearly upright, but
bend a little from the ftem, by which attitude
the upper part of the corolla fhelters the parts
of the fructification. None of thefe plants are
poifonous, but many of them are admired for
their odoriferous fmell and kitchen ufes, as well
as for the medicinal qualities which fome of
them poffefs. A cup, divided into five clefts,
is a circumftance in which the following plants
of this order generally agree: Motherwort *,
Ground Ivy †, Mint ‡, Germander §, Bugle ‖,
Betony ¶, Dead Nettle **, Catmint ††, Hen-
bit ‡‡, Horehound §§; but Thyme ‖‖, Self-

---

* Leonorus.   † Gleckma.   ‡ Mentha.   § Teucrium.
‖ Ajuga.   ¶ Betonica.   ** Glanium.   †† Nepeta.
‡‡ Ballota.   §§ Marrubium.   ‖‖ Thymus.

heal,

heal *, Marjoram †, Bafil ‡, Balm-leaf §, and
Calamint ‖, have their calyxes cleft into two
parts.   Small fwellings are frequently found
upon the leaves of the Ground Ivy, which are
occafioned by an infect; if opened, they are obferved to be compofed of many cells.   In Mint,
the ftamens are diftant, upright, and one pair
longer than the other; but thofe of the Water-
Mint are all nearly of the fame length.   The
upper lip of the bloffom of the Germander is
deeply divided, and the parts gaping widely
afunder, gives it the appearance of wanting that
part of the corolla.   The flowers of one fpecies
of the Bugle grow in the form of a four-fided
pyramid befet with hairs.   Betony has the upper
lip circular, entire, flat, and upright; the lower
one divided into three fegments; the middle
ones notched at the end.   Wood Betony has the
root-leaves on leaf-ftalks, the others, heart-fhaped and fitting clofe to the ftem, the flowers grow
in an interrupted fpike.   The red Dead Nettle,
though a weed regarded with contempt, is a
pleafing ornament to the banks of ditches in the
early part of fummer.   Its bloffoms, of a reddifh
purple, grow in whorls, confifting of many
flowers, on the tops of the ftems, which being
interfected with green leaves, gives it a pretty

* Prunella.   † Origanum.   ‡ Clinopodium.   § Melittis.
‖ Meliffa.

appearance

appearance. The conftru&ion of the cup in the
Hooded Willowherb is deferving of peculiar
remark : the rim is almoft entire, covered by a
fcale lying over it like a lid, when the bloffom
falls off, the cup clofes upon the feeds, which
would remain fhut up without poffibility of
efcape ; but the cup withers and divides into
two feparate parts, and by that means affords the
feeds an opportunity of falling to the ground,
and producing young plants the next feafon.
Thyme is another of thofe which have the cup
bilabiate, or cloven into two lips; the ftems of
the Common Thyme are woody; the Bafil
Thyme is diftinguifhed by the middle fegment
of the lower lip of the corolla being notched,
and marked with a raifed white fpot in the fhape
of a crefcent. The generic chara&er of Self-
heal, confifts in its forked ftamens, the tips fixed
to the threads beneath the top, and adhering
only to one of the divifions of the fork.   In
open funny fituations, it trails; but grows upright, a foot high, in woods. Marjoram is known
by a fpiked fence. The flowers grow in roundifh fpikes, the leaves oval, and pointed, are produced on leaf ftalks, the bloffoms are purple.·
The whole plant is a warm aromatic, and is
found among brambles and hedges in the month
of July. Let us proceed to the fecond order,
which you may recolle& is diftinguifhed from

the

the firſt, by the ſeeds of all the genera being incloſed in a pericarp or capſule. The number of
ſegments in the cup varies: in ſome, it is divided
into two parts, in others four, and in many five.
The corollas of the firſt order are almoſt all of
them labiate or ringent, but in thoſe of the
order under notice, many of them are perſonate,
or have the lips cloſed. Broomrape * has a
cup, with either two or five clefts, a gaping corolla, with four ſegments nearly equal, and a
gland at the baſe of the ſeed-bud, for the purpoſe
of ſecreting the honey. A downy undivided
ſtem, and the ſtamens appearing above the bloſſom, diſtinguiſh the common kind. Tooth-
wort †, Paintedcup ‡, Eyebright §, Rattle ‖, and
Cowwheat ¶ are among thoſe whoſe cups are
cloven into four ſegments. The capſule of the
firſt is roundiſh, but terminates in a ſmall point,
it has one cell and two elaſtic valves, ſurrounded
by the cup, which is large and expanding. The
Paintedcup is diſtinguiſhed by its coloured cup
from the Rattle, the Eyebright, and the Louſe-
wort, between which it forms a ſort of connect-
ing link. The Yellow Rattle has the edges of
the capſule bordered with a kind of margin, and
the ſeeds incloſed in a looſe membrane ; when
they are ripe they make a rattling noiſe in the

---

* Orobanche.   † Lathræa.   ‡ Bartſia.   § Euphraſia.
‖ Rinanthus.   ¶ Melampyrum.

capſule.

capfule. There is a variety with very narrow leaves, the bloſſoms of which are yellow with purple lips. The ſtalk of the Eyebright is much branched and ſquare, the branches oppo-ſite to each other, the leaves ſitting on the ſtem, thoſe neareſt the flowers ſometimes purpliſh; the flowers of a duſky red, growing in ſpikes, inclined all one way, and nodding at the top. The tips of the ſtamens are pointed with a thorn or ſpine, at the baſe of the lower lobe, and the capſule is divided into two cells. The corolla of the Figwort * has a large globular tube, with a very narrow border, divided into five ſeg-ments; the two upper ones erect, and larger than the reſt, thoſe on the ſides ſpread open, and the lower one turned back; in ſome ſpecies, there is another ſmall ſegment, lying like a flap under the uppermoſt diviſion. The common yellow Toadflax † grows very commonly upon banks by road ſides, which it embelliſhes with its beautiful heads of flowers, growing upon an erect ſtalk, thickly beſet with long narrow leaves of a bluiſh colour; the under lip of the corolla is hairy within, and, by projecting, cloſes the mouth the chaps are orange coloured, but the reſt of a pale yellow, the bloſſom terminates in a long ſpur. Although the Toadflax has great claim to admiration for its beauty, it is far ex-

---

* Scrophularia.　　† Antirrhinum.

celled

celled by the Purple Foxglove *, which is one of the moſt ſplendid flowers that grow wild in this country. The ſtem riſes from three to ſix feet high, and is adorned with pendulous bell-ſhaped flowers, hanging one above another in a very long ſpike: they are of a fine purple, elegantly mottled withinſide with ſpots like eyes; the ſegments of the calyx are of an oval pointed ſhape, and the leaves large and wrinkled. Mrs. Snelgrove waits for me, to accompany her to gather flowers, to fill the vaſes in the hall. I ſhall be no longer confined to the humble productions of the field or the hedge, but ſhall indulge my taſte, in compoſing a garland from among the richeſt of Flora's beauties. Adieu! Adieu!

FELICIA.

LETTER XX.

WITH pleaſure do I retire from other company, to devote an hour to the agreeable employment of chatting with you, and renewing bota-

* Digitalis.

nica*l*

nical topics. Suppofe me feated in our dreffing room, with many fpecimens before me of the clafs Tetradynamia, which is known by the fame number of ftamens as the fixth clafs, in which they are all nearly of equal length : but, in the fifteenth, which we are now going to examine, four of them are longer than the other two. The form of the feed-veffel divides the plants of this clafs into two orders; the firft called Siliculofa, comprifes thofe that have a a fhort roundifh pod or pouch for a feed-veffel ; frequently furnifhed with a fhaft, in fome kinds as long as the pouch itfelf. This order is naturally fubdivided into thofe which have a notch at the top of the filicle or pouch, and thofe which are entire. In the fecond order, called Siliquofa, the feeds are contained in a long flender pod. The natural charaƈter of thefe flowers correfponds fo exaƈtly with my defcription of the Stock Gilliflower in a former letter, that I fhall only refer you to that, without enlarging on particulars, and teafing you with a repetition of what I have already told you. Whitlowgrafs*, Awlwort†, Camline‡, and Creffet §, are among thofe which have the feed-veffel entire ; the firft has its feeds contained in a fhort oval flat pod, without any fhaft : it is a diminutive plant, and flowers very early. Awlwort has an

* Draba.   † Subularia.   ‡ Myagrum.   § Vella.

egg-

egg-fhaped pouch furnifhed with a very fhort fhaft. It is found at the bottom of large lakes. Camline, called by the country people Gold of Pleafure, has alfo an egg-fhaped pouch, with a permanent fhaft. The pouch in Creffet is of a globular form. The Shepherd's Purfe * is a familiar example of the fecond fubdivifion. You need not go far out of your way in fearch of it, for it grows almoft every where; the proper feafon for its flowering is in the months of March and April, but its bloffoms are feen nearly the year round. The foil, from whence it derives its nourifhment, has great influence, both upon its height and the fhape of the leaves; in fome places it is no more than three inches high, in others it reaches to as many feet. It has obtained its name from the fhape of its pods, which are ·like an inverted heart, deeply notched at top, and obvioufly diftinguifhing it from the others among which it ranks.

The fecond order is alfo feparated into two fections; in the firft, the leaves of the cup approach each other towards the top, clofing the cup; in the fecond, they diverge or fpread wide open. Wormfeed †, Turkey-pod ‡, Wallflower §, and Cabbage ||, are among the former. The pod in Wormfeed is long and narrow,

---

* Thlafpi.   † Eryfimum.   ‡ Arabis.   § Cheiranthus.
|| Braffica

with

with four edges; the common fort is known by
the pods growing clofe to the fpike. Winter-
Creffes, another fpecies, has lyre-fhaped leaves,
with a circular fegment at the end; and a third
fort, called Jack by the Hedge, or Sauce-alone,
from its fmell refembling Garlick, has leaves of an
heart fhape and white bloffoms. Turkey-pod
is furnifhed with four honey-cups, each compofed of a fmall reflex fcale, fixed to the bottom
of the receptacle, within the leaflets of the calyx. The Moufe-ear, one of the fpecies, has
white bloffoms, and the leaves fitting clofe to
the ftem. Cultivation has produced many beautiful varieties of the Wallflower, both double
and fingle, differing in colour from the pale
yellow to the deep orange; but none of them
excelling the wild kind in fragrance. The bafe
of each of the fhort ftamens is furrounded by a
honey-cup gland, that caufes the hunched appearance of the cup, which you may have remarked. Both Cabbage and Turnip have four
honey-cups, one placed between each fhort ftamen and the pointal, and one between each pair
of the longer ftamens and the cup; the leaflets
which form the calyx are erect, and the claws
of the petals nearly as long as the cup; the pod
is fhaped like a cylinder flattened at the fides,
having valves not fo long as the partition, and
containing feveral globular feeds: thus far they
agree,

agree ; but the root of the Turnip differs materially from that of the Cabbage ; it is a continu-
ation of the ftem, forming that round, compreffed, flefhy fubftance which we eat, and which
affords wholefome nourifhment to cattle as well
as man.   In the fecond feftion we fhall find Sea-
Colewort *, Woad †, Muftard ‡, and Water-
Crefs §.   The effential charafter of the firft
depends upon the four longer filaments being
forked, and the anthers fixed on the outer forks.
Woad has a fpear-fhaped oblong pod, with one
cell and two valves, which are boat-fhaped ; in
the centre of the feed-veffel is one feed only.
That fpecies, which has the root leaves fcolloped,
and thofe on the ftem arrow-fhaped, with yellow
bloffoms, was ufed formerly by the ancient Britons to ftain their bodies, in order to render
them more formidable to their enemies, by their
terrific appearance ; it has fince been found of
extenfive utility in the art of dyeing, forming
the bafis of many colours, particularly blue.
Muftard differs from Cabbage, although nearly
allied to it, in having an expanding cup and the
claws of the petals upright.   In both, the honey-
cup glands are placed in a fimilar manner.   The
pod is rough, and the partition ufually much
longer than the valves.   One fpecies, abounding in corn fields, has a fmooth pod, with many

---

* Crambe.   † Ifatis.   ‡ Sinapis.   § Sifymbrium.

angles,

angles, bunched out by the feeds. The leaves are harſh and deeply indented, the bloſſom it bears is yellow, which produces brown feeds. The common ſort, with whoſe feeds, reduced to powder, we uſe to feaſon our food, has alſo a ſmooth pod, the lower leaves are large and harſh, but the upper ones ſmooth and without indentures, not only the bloſſom is yellow, but the cup alſo. The Water-Creſs, ſo well known for the wholeſome and pleaſant ſallad it affords, is moſtly found in running waters, ſuch as brooks and rivulets. The corolla, as well as the calyx, is expanding in this numerous genus, and the valves of the feed-veſſel are ſtraight and ſhorter than the partition. The charaĉters that diſtinguiſh the common ſpecies, are pods declining, and wing-ſhaped leaves with white bloſſoms, which grow in a corymb. Having given you a ſufficient number of examples in this claſs, to ſpur your induſtry to ſearch for more, I ſhall bring my letter to a concluſion, and take the advantage of a fine afternoon to enjoy a diſh of tea with my mother in the ſummerhouſe. How I wiſh you could be of the party! that addition would complete the pleaſure of your truly affectionate ſiſter,

FELICIA.

LETTER

LETTER XXI.

DEAR SISTER,   *Shrubbery, July 9.*

AS the feafon is ftealing on us apace, I am impatient of delay, being defirous of conducting
you through all the twenty-four claffes of Linnæus before you return; next fummer I promife myfelf the pleafure of recapitulating our
firft principles, and applying them to new objects together, which will give us an opportunity
of trying our ftrength, and confirming what little
knowledge we may have acquired. We are
now arrived at the fixteenth clafs, which differs,
in many refpects, from any that we have hitherto confidered. In all the preceding ones you
may have obferved, that the ftamens, whether
few or many, have been evidently diftinct from
each other; but in the prefent inftance, you
will always find them united at bottom, into one
brotherhood, as it is called, and that is the mean-
ing of the Greek name Monodelphìa; but ftill
they are perfectly feparate at top, which is a
diftinction that characterifes this clafs from fome
fucceeding ones. The number of ftamens being
unneceffary to determine the clafs, is ufed for a
different purpofe, and the orders are arranged
according

according to the number of them in each flower. The features by which this natural tribe is recognifed, are a cup that is permanent, and, in many inftances, double; a corolla compofed of five petals, fhaped like a heart reverfed, the edge of one lying over that of the next, in an oppofite direction to the apparent motion of the fun; the anthers fixed fideways to the filaments, which are of unequal lengths, the outer ones being the fhorteft; the receptacle rifes in the midft of the flower like a column, the top of it encircled by the upright feed-buds, in the form of a jointed ring; all the pointals are united at their bafe into one body with the receptacle, though divided at top into as many parts as there are feed-buds; thefe feed-buds become capfules, the number of the cells are regulated by the number of the pointals, the figure varies in different genera, and they frequently confift of as many feed-coats or arils, each concealing a kidney-fhaped feed. Decandria, fo denominated from having ten ftamens, is the firft order of which I fhall treat; it comprehends but one genus of thofe plants that grow wild in Great Britain, but that is a very numerous one, and is known by the name of Cranefbill *; the beautiful family of Geraniums, of which our greenhoufe difplays fuch an amazing variety, is of the fame genus;

* Geranium.

but

but as moſt of theſe came originally from the
Cape of Good Hope, I ſhall leave them to your
own examination, and proceed to ſeleƈt a few
native ſpecimens. The circumſtances common
to the different ſpecies, are a ſingle cup of five
leaves, the petals of the corolla correſponding
with them in number; the ten ſtamens alternately longer and ſhorter, but all of them ſhorter
than the bloſſom; one pointal terminated by five
ſtigmas, longer than the ſtamens, and permanent
as well as the cup; the fruit compoſed of five
dry berries furniſhed with a bill, each containing a ſingle ſeed, crowned with a tail or awn,
which rolls up in a ſpiral form when the ſeed
becomes ripe; and thus they are detached from
the flower, and ſcattered about, in order to pre-
ſerve the ſpecies. Every other ſtamen, only, is
furniſhed with a tip in ſome ſpecies. The awn
of the ſeed is ſometimes hairy, and in other inſtances ſmooth. The Hemlock-leaved Cranes-
bill, as well as the muſked, has but five ſtamens,
in both the leaves are winged and jagged at the
edges, and ſeveral flowers grow on the ſame
foot-ſtalk, but the latter is known by a ſtrong
ſmell of muſk, which it loſes upon being bruiſed.
In the next ſeƈtion are found ten ſtamens, all
tipped with anthers, and the fruit-ſtalks ſupporting two flowers. The ſpotted Cranesbill has
downy leaves, with five lobes or ſcollops, and
theſe

thefe again divided into fmaller indentures; the bloffoms are of a deep purple. In the Meadow Cranefbill they are of a fine blue, the petals are entire, and the leaves are wrinkled and divided deeply into many parts. In woods, and efpecially under the hedges which furround woods, is frequently found the herb Robert, which loves a fhady, fheltered fituation, the ftalks are as red as blood, and, towards the end of the year, both ftalks and leaves become of the fame colour. It is diftinguifhed from others of the fame genus, by its hairy pointed cups, with ten angles; the bloffoms are of a pale rofe-colour, though fometimes a variety occurs with white ones. Many ftamens in one flower charaƈterife the fixth order. Lavatera, or Velvet-leaf, has a double cup, one leaf with three fhallow clefts, forms the outer one, the inner one is alfo of one leaf, but divided into five clefts, the feed-coats compofe a ring round the receptacle, which ftands like a pillar in the centre of the bloffom; the fpecies, found here, has a woody ftem and downy plaited leaves, with feven angles; it grows on the feafhore. The ftem of the Dwarf Mallow is proftrate, the leaves circular and flightly indented, the fruit-ftalks declining. Before the art of gardening had attained the perfeƈtion of modern times, the leaves of this plant was brought to table, as thofe of the cabbage are at prefent.

G   The

The common kind, which abounds in hedges, foot-paths, and amongſt rubbiſh, has an upright ſtem, the leaves have ſeven ſharp diviſions, both foot-ſtalks and leaf ſtalks are hairy. It is often cultivated, and many varieties produced. The Marſhmallow * is marked by its ſimple downy leaves, as ſoft as velvet, the bloſſom reſembles that of the Mallow. It is valued for its medicinal, healing qualities, being generally uſeful as an external application, in thoſe caſes where cooling, ſoftening remedies are neceſſary. Before you diſmiſs the Mallow tribe, take your microſcope, and examine the duſt of the anthers ; it will afford you entertainment, being curiouſly toothed like the wheels of a watch. The moſt minute parts of nature are finiſhed with an elegant nicety, that ſurpaſſes the utmoſt efforts of art. The finger of the Divine Artiſt is viſible in the moſt minute of his works ; let us be excited to obſerve them with the greateſt attention, they will not only ſupply us with preſent amuſement and wonder, but will ſerve as a hidden treaſure to alleviate the ſolitude and weariſomeneſs of old age. May a ſimiliarity of taſte and ſentiment continue to unite us in the ſame purſuits, to the end of our days.

FELICIA.

* Althæa.

LETTER

LETTER XXII.

DEAR CONSTANCE,   *Shrubbery, July* 14.

THE leguminous plants, or Butterfly-ſhaped
flowers, are comprehended in the ſeventeenth
claſs, Diadelphia. The diſpoſition of the ſtamens diſtinguiſhes the claſs, and the number of
them the orders. In the firſt order there are
five, in the ſecond ſix, in the third eight, and in
the fourth ten. The ſignification of the Greek
name, is two brotherhoods; and you might ex-
pect, from that circumſtance, to find them always
divided into two ſets; but this is not invariably
the caſe, for, in many inſtances, they are united
in one ſet only. The natural character you
have already ſtudied pretty attentively, under the
deſcription of the Pea flower, which will ſerve
to give a general idea of all the reſt. The three
firſt orders will furniſh me with only two genera
for your inſpection. Fumitory * has but two filaments, each of them crowned by three anthers,
which is ſufficient to place it in the ſecond order.
It has a cup of two leaves, and the bloſſom par-
takes more of the form of the ringent than the
papilionaceous flowers; the upper lip, however,

* Fumaria.

G 2   correſponds

correfponds to the banner, the lower one to the
keel, and the cloven mouth to the wings. Common Fumitory bears the feed-veffels in bunches,
each containing a fingle feed : the leaves are
doubly winged, with three divifions, and thefe
again fubdivided. The bloffoms are produced
in long fpikes, at the end of the ftalks, ard are of
a pink and deep purple. There is but one fpecies
of Milkwort *, though the genus is numerous,
which grows without culture, and that is found on
heaths and poor meadow ground. It is ranked
in the third order, Octandria, on account of its
eight filaments, each being tipped with anthers,
which are united at the bottom. The wings may
be faid to belong to the cup, as they are formed of two coloured leaves which proceed from it.
The banner is generally cylindrical ; towards the
end of the keel, which is hollow, are fixed two
appendages, pencil fhaped, with three divifions ;
many fpecies are without this diftinction, which
throws the genus naturally into two fections.
The flowers of the wild fort are furnifhed with
this creft, they grow in bunches on herbaceous
ftems, which are trailing ; the leaves are narrow,
and the mixture of blue, white, and flefh-colour-
ed bloffoms has a pretty effect. The plants of
the laft order are numerous, and bear fuch an
affinity, in their general appearance, that it is not

* Polygala.

difficult

difficult to recognife them at firft fight. The
papilionaceous bloſſom, the leaves moſtly in
pairs, like wings, up the leaf-ſtalks, ſometimes
terminated by a fingle one; ſtalks ſlender and
creeping, unable to ſuppori themſelves, and
twiſting round every thing near them. Frequently furniſhed with tendrils or claſps, for the
purpoſe of holding by the firſt prop they can
reach, are features that denote them to belong
to the ſame family. But this air or charaɛter
muſt always be confirmed by the union of the
ten filaments at the bottom, which puts the
matter beyond doubt; remembering what I
have already obſerved, that, although the eſſential mark of the claſs is the ſeparation of the
ſtamens into two ſets, nine of them incloſed together by a membrane ſurrounding the germ,
and the tenth placed by itſelf above the pointal,
yet in many ſpecies they grow all ten together,
which muſt not deter you from arranging them
amongſt their proper companions. Several
trees and ſhrubs are found with Butterfly ſhaped
bloſſoms, and poſſeſſing the requiſites of the
claſs, are ranked in it. Among the ſhrubs are
the Broom * and the Geniſta, adorning the
hedges of dry paſtures by their ſhowy yellow
flowers, the ten ſtamens are conneɛted in both,
the leaves of the former grow in threes, and the

* Spartium.

G 3   branches

branches are without prickles; in the latter, the
leaves are gloffy, narrow, and upright, and the
branches ftreaked. You can fcarcely pafs over
a heath or common that is not covered with
Gorze*, or Furze, which differs from the Broom
and Genifta, in having a cup with two leaves,
and the legume fo fhort, as to be almoft covered
by it. This is an extremely hardy fhrub, and,
on that account, is fuitable for fences in the
bleakeft fituations; not even the fea-fpray de-
ftroys it, which kills almoft every other. A calyx, with five divifions, nearly as long as the
bloffom, and the ten filaments united in one entire cylinder, diftinguifh the Reftharrows †,
which are lowly fhrubs, growing alfo on heaths
and barren places. The Dutch fow them on
the banks of their dykes, as their ftrong matted
roots tend to fortify them againft the incurfions
of the water. The Wood Pea ‡ has a calyx of
one leaf, the ftandard of the corolla reflected
back, the wings approaching and rifing upwards;
nine of the filaments are united beneath the
pointal, but the tenth is placed above it, and af-
cends upwards. It is an elegant plant, the ftem
fimple below, but branched towards the top,
bearing three or four purple bloffoms on a
branch, which become blue as they go off, and
are fucceeded by a legume, which likewife

* Ulex.   † Ononis.   ‡ Orobus.

changes

changes from red to black : the feparation of
the branches are cloathed with half arrow-fhaped
props, often jagged at the bottom. The High-
landers dry the roots, and chew them like to-
bacco, to repel hunger and thirft. The chief
diftinction between the Pea* and the Vetchling†
confifts in the fhaft ; in the Pea it is triangular,
keel-fhaped, and woolly ; whilft that of the
Vetchling is flat and upright, with a woolly
fummit. Some fpecies produce only one flower
on a foot-ftalk, among which are the Yellow
Vetchling and Crimfon Grafs Vetch, the former
having tendrils without leaves, and props fhaped
like the head of an arrow ; the latter has fimple
leaves, and awl-fhaped props. Some others bear
feveral flowers on a fruit-ftalk, as the Rough-
codded Chickling Vetch, which has fpear-fhaped
leaves, with hairy fhells and rough feeds. The
bloffoms are crimfon, ftreaked with yellow lines
withinfide. In the fame divifion are the broad
and narrow-leaved Peafe everlafting : they agree
in having tendrils furnifhed with two leaves,
which in the one do not exceed the breadth of the
ftem ; but in the other are much broader. The
Vetch‡, or Tare, is marked by having the ftigma
of the pointal bearded on the under fide, the filaments are divided into two fets, and the genus
into two fections, the firft bearing the flowers on

---

* Pifum.   † Lathyrus.   ‡ Vicia.

peduncles, the fecond producing them at the bafe of the leaves, fitting almoft clofe to the ftem. Of the former fection are two fpecies, one with little oval leaves and white bloffoms, the other with fpear-fhaped downy leaves and purple bloffoms. Among thofe of the fecond fection, one generally produces two legumes growing together, another four, and in a third fort they grow fingle. There are many fpecies of the Trefoils*, their flowers forming a little rundle or head upon a common receptacle; the wings of the corolla are fhorter than the ftandards, which is reflected, and the keel ftill fhorter than the wings. The fubterranean Trefoil takes its name from its fhells being frequently produced under the furface of the earth, the heads are woolly, containing five flowers, with a bufhy fubftance in the middle, involving the feed-veffel. It was not known to be a native of this country till very lately. In the autumn of 1795 it was found at Norwich and Languard Fort. Saintfoin † is cultivated like clover for feeding cattle. It loves a dry chalky foil; the leaves are winged, and the fhells covered with prickles, each fhell containing a fingle feed. The effential character of the Horfefhoe ‡ confifts in the form of the fhell, whence it takes its name. The fhape of the legume particularifes

* Trifolium.   † Hedyfarum.   ‡ Hippocrepis.

the

the different fpecies of Snail-fhell *, in fome it
is rolled up fpirally, like the fhell of a fnail, or a
green caterpillar; in others it is of a femicircular
form refembling a bow or a crefcent. Shall I
intrude, my dear Conftance, by introducing the
next clafs before I clofe my letter, as it contains
but one genus natural to this country : I am un-
willing to appropriate a letter to it only, trufting
to your ufual patience to forgive me, if I weary
you. The circumftance of the ftamens being
united by the threads into three or more fets,
gives the name of Polyadelphia to the eighteenth
clafs. The only genus I fhall mention is the
Tutfan †, which has a cup with five divifions,
inclofing the feed-bud, and a bloffom of five petals, bending from the left to the right, its numerous hair-like threads connected at bottom,
into three or five fets, like a hair pencil with
fmall tips; the fhafts vary in number, from one
or two, to five; the feed-veffel is a capfule, with
as many cells as there are fhafts. Park-leaves,
or Tutfan St. John's Wort, has three pointals,
its bloffoms are yellow, which are fucceeded by
a berry, the ftem is fhrubby and two edged.
Common St. John's Wort has the fame number
of pointals, and a ftem refembling that of the
laft mentioned kind but it differs from it in its
leaves, which are blunt and fprinkled with tran-

* Medicago.　　† Hypericum.

G 5　　　　　　　fparent

fparent fpots, that are fometimes red; another
fpecies has proftrate, trailing ftems, the flowers
growing fingly at the bafe of the leaves. Among
hedges and on rough grounds, is found the hairy
St. John's Wort, with upright cylindrical ftems,
and downy egg-fhaped leaves. Adieu! I perceive the approaches of autumn with pleafure,
confidering them as forerunners of that period,
which is fixed for your return to your affectionate

FELICIA.

LETTER XXIII.

Shrubbery, Auguft 5.

RECAL to your mind, my dear Conftance,
what I formerly told you of the compound
flowers, defcribed in the fyftem of Linnæus, in
the general account of the nineteenth clafs, Syngenefia. Before I proceed to point out the peculiarities of the different genera, it is neceffary
to acquire pretty accurate ideas of the ftructure
of the parts which compofe the different kinds

of

of compound flowers, as well as the diftinctions of the orders into which the clafs is divided. The effential character of a compound flower does not confift in the compofition of many florets, but in the union of the tips at top, into the form of a cylinder, and a fingle feed being placed upon the receptacle under each floret. Though the flowers of this clafs generally are compofed of many florets fitting upon a common receptacle, inclofed by one common empalement. Sometimes this calyx confifts of a fingle row of fcales or leaves, divided to the bafe, for the convenience of clofing or opening without tearing; in other genera, the fcales are numerous, lying one above another in rows, like the tiles upon the roof of a houfe, whilft the cups of fome are formed of a row of equal fegments next to the florets, and another row of fhort fcales grow at the bafe of the longer ones, and turn back towards the foot-ftalk. The furface of the receptacle is of different forms, concave, flat, convex, pyramidal, or globular, and is either fmooth, full of little holes, or befet with foft hairs, or fmall upright fcales, which feparate the florets placed upon it. A floret confifts of one petal, moftly regular, and the border divided into three clefts; the five filaments of the ftamens are fixed to the tube of this corolla, and unite at top, fo as to form a cylindrical tube, through

which

which paffes the fhaft of the pointal, the fummit
moftly rifing above the floret, and terminating
in two curling forks. The floret and pointal
both reft upon the feed-bud, which lengthens as
the feed becomes mature; if it be a naked feed,
it falls to the ground, when ripe; but if winged,
or tipped with feathers, it wafts its way through
the air to a diftance, and there produces a new
plant the following feafon. This downy fubftance, or crown of feathers, is either fitting
clofe to the feed, or fixed on the top of a pedicle, like a fmall pillar. The natural tribe, under
confideration, will furnifh you with much fubject of admiration, and bring new proofs to your
reflecting mind, that thofe parts of organifed
nature, which appear, to a cafual obferver, as tri-
vial and infignificant, are contrived with the
moft perfect wifdom and intelligence, and with
defign to anfwer particular purpofes. Who can
obferve without wonder, the elafticity of the
calyx in many genera of this clafs? The expanfion of the florets appears to burft it open, but
when they wither, it rifes up and clofes, by
which means the tender feed is protected, till it
is fit for difperfion; the hairs that crown the
feeds, before upright, diverge, and force the
leaves of the calyx open again, which now bend
quite back, and leave a paffage for the feeds to
efcape. For the diftinction of the orders, I muft
refer

refer you to my eighth letter. The order Polygamia Æqualis is fubdivided into three fections.
In the firft, all the florets are narrow, or correfponding with the Semiflofculous flowers of
Tournefort; in the next, the flowers grow in
globular heads; and the third is compofed of
thofe which have tubular florets only. Endive *
has a double cup, the receptacle a little chaffy,
and the feather five toothed. The blofloms of
the wild Succory or Endive are blue, and grow
in pairs fitting on the ftem; the leaves are
notched. Goatfbeard †, Oxtongue ‡, and Dandelion §, agree in having a naked receptacle and
a downy feather; but the cup in Goatfbeard is
fimple, compofed of eight fpear-fhaped leaves;
thofe of the plant are entire, ftiff, and ftraight.
This is one of Flora's time-keepers: the bloffom expands early in the morning, and clofes
again before noon. Oxtongue has a double cup
and a yellow bloffom. The empalement in the
Dandelion is tiled, the leaves are deeply jagged,
the round white heads formed by the expanfion
of the downy feathers you are too well acquainted with, to need a defcription, as they have fo
often amufed our infant hours with blowing
them off the receptacle. The fecond fection
prefents us with the Thiftle ‖ tribe, difregarded

* Cichorium. † Tragopogon. ‡ Picris. § Leontodon.
‖ Carduus.

on

on account of their uncouth, harſh appearance,
and their abundance, but neither deſtitute of
beauty, on further inſpe&ion, or void of utility ;
for nothing would grow for years on clay newly
thrown up, were it not that the ſeeds of thiſtles
fix and vegetate there, and, as they grow up,
ſhelter other plants, which arrive at maturity
under their prote&ion.   Many of the ſpecies
have latterly been introduced into gardens, and
become beautiful by cultivation.   An empalement, beſet with thorny ſcales, and a receptacle
with hairs between the ſeeds chara&eriſe this
intra&able race.   The leaves of many of the
ſpecies run along the ſtem, their thorny edges
forbid a very cloſe approach.   The Milk Thiſtle
has the leaves prettily marbled with white, they
are halberd-ſhaped, with thorny winged clefts.
The banks of rivers and brooks will afford you the
Liverhemp*, as a ſpecimen of the third ſe&ion ;
a large plant with fingered leaves, the ſtalks are tall
and rough, and bear bunches of pale red bloſſoms,
each cup containing about five florets.   The
genus is known by a tiled oblong cup, a naked
receptacle, a downy feather, and a very long
pointal, cloven down to the ſtamens.   The ſecond order, Polygamia Superflua, is divided into
two ſe&ions; the firſt containing thoſe that have
all the florets tubular ; the ſecond, thoſe that are

* Eupatorium.

radiate,

radiate, and in which the florets of the circumference are narrow or ſtrap-ſhaped. The genus
Artemiſia includes Southernwood, the Worm-
woods, and Mugwort, each of which poſſeſs the
quality of an aromatic bitter. They are known
by a roundiſh empalement, compoſed of many
circular ſcales, naked ſeeds, and a flat receptacle,
which is either woolly or bare; the flowers are
entirely without a ray, and conſequently exem-
plify thoſe called diſcoid. Wild Southernwood
has leaves with many clefts, and long tender
ſhoots proceeding from its trailing ſtems. The
Common Wormwood is diſtinguiſhed from it
by upright herbaceous ſtems; the flowers are
rather globular and pendant, the leaves are compound, with many diviſions; the bloſſoms of
both are browniſh, a colour unuſual among
flowers. Nature appears to delight in diſplaying
the gayeſt hues in the vegetable part of the creation. Tanſey *, with the juice of which pud-
dings are frequently flavoured, has an empalement, ſhaped like a globe, divided in half, tiled
with ſharp ſcales; the flowers of the ray have
only three clefts, but thoſe of the diſk five; both
the ſeeds and the receptacle are naked. The
common Tanſey bears yellow bloſſoms, the
leaves are doubly winged, and jagged at the
edges. The fleſh-fly has ſuch a diſlike to the

* Tanacetum.

ſmell

ſmell of this plant, that any animal ſubſtance, ſuch as meat, &c. that is rubbed with it, is per-fectly ſecure from the attacks of this inſect. The Daiſy*, which enamels every meadow with its vernal and autumnal flowers, belongs to the ſecond diviſion; the cup is formed of a double row of ſmall ſpear-ſhaped leaves; the numerous tubular florets in the diſk are furniſhed with both ſtamens and pointals, whilſt thoſe which com-poſe the ray are ſtrap-ſhaped, and contain point-als only: the ſeeds are without a feather, and the receptacle naked and conical. Apply your microſcope, and you will be pleaſed with the beauty and variety diſcernible in this little diſ-regarded flower. The florets of the centre are yellow, thoſe of the ray white above and pink beneath; the leaves of the common ſort are ob-long and blunt, and ſpread flat upon the ground, a naked ſtalk ſupports a ſingle flower. Both Chamomile † and Yarrow ‡ have chaffy recep-tacles, but the calyx of the firſt is hemiſpherical, or of the ſhape of a globe divided in half, whilſt that of the latter is oblong or egg-ſhaped, and tiled with ſharp ſcales. Chamomile has more than five ſemiflorets in the ray, and the ſeeds are without down. The ſpecies that is uſed me-dicinally, as well as ſeveral other ſpecies, has yellow florets in the centre, ſurrounded by white

* Bellis.   † Anthemis.   ‡ Achillea.

ones

ones in the circumference, the leaves are winged
and compound, with fharp narrow divifions, the
whole a little hairy : cultivation renders it
double, by increafing the number of the florets
in the circumference, and diminifhing thofe of
the centre. The leaves of the common Yarrow
are doubly winged and without hairs, the ftem is
furrowed towards the top, it bears a white bloffom, fometimes tinged with red or purple.
Were I to enumerate all the genera of this numerous order, I fhould extend my letter to an
unreafonable length, therefore you muft be contented with thofe already noticed, and fuffer me
to proceed to the third order, from which I fhall
felect only the Knapweed *. In this genus the
fcales of the cup and the feathers of the feed
vary in different fpecies ; the corollas of the ray
are tubular, longer than thofe of the difk, and
irregular in their form ; the receptacle is furnifhed with briftles between the florets. There
are many varieties of the Blue-bottle or Corn-
flower, if we enumerate them by the colour of
the bloffom, which is fometimes white, red,
purple, violet, or variegated with different hues ;
but, in all, the fcales of the cup are fringed, the
upper leaves are narrow and entire, but thofe towards the ground are broader, and toothed at the
edges. Great Knapweed has leaves with wing-

* Centaurea.

ed

ed clefts, and bears its bloſſoms on long naked
fruit-ſtalks ; another ſpecies called Horſe-knops,
has ſkinny, ragged cups, with ſpear-ſhaped leaves
and angular branches : there are two other ſpecies
with cups doubly ſpined, one of them called Star-
thiſtle, has ſtrap-ſhaped toothed leaves with winged clefts and a hairy ſtem. St. Barnaby's Thiſtle
is known by its ſpear-ſhaped leaves running
along the branches, thoſe neareſt the root are
lyre-ſhaped and winged. The generic characters of Cudweed*, the only ſpecimen I ſhall
mention of the fourth order are, a naked receptacle, ſeeds without down, and florets with pointals fixed amongſt the ſcales of the calyx. Barren paſtures and ſandy corn fields produce the
different ſpecies, which are chiefly diſtinguiſhed
by the form of the flowers : in one kind they are
round, in a ſecond conical, and in a third awl-
ſhaped. The ſixth and laſt order differs widely
from the natural family of compound flowers,
contained in thoſe of the preceding orders, except in the union of the five anthers, the appropriate badge of the claſs. The flowers are ſimple ; that is to ſay, one flower is incloſed in one
calyx, like thoſe of the other claſſes. The
whole genus of Violets† is furniſhed with a cup
of five leaves, an irregular corolla of five petals,
the uppermoſt petal terminating at the baſe in a

* Filago.   † Viola.

horn

horn or fpur, performing the office of a nectary
or honey-cup, and a capfule of one cell and
three valves, above the receptacle, or inclofed
by the calyx. The Sweet Violet, fo much valued and admired for its odoriferous fragrance,
perfuming the banks and hedges in fpring, is
among thofe which have no ftalk, but that which
fupports the flower, and the fuckers which creep
from it ; the leaves are heart-fhaped, and the
bloffoms darkifh purple ; there is a variety with
white flowers : the colour, as well as the number of the petals, is varied by cultivation, confequently this vernal favourite is feen in gardens under many appearances. At the fiıft
opening of the Dog Violet, it has no ftalk; but,
as it attains its full growth, the ftalk fhoots up
and produces both fruit-ftalks and leaves, which
fufficiently diftinguifhes it from the Sweet Violet, whofe leaves grow only from the root.
Hearts Eafe, or Panfies, have props with winged
clefts and a globular, open, hollow ftigma, fringed towards the bottom ; the ftems are fpreading
and three-cornered, with oblong gafhed leaves :
it obtains its name of Tricolor, from the union of
purple, yellow, and light blue, which enriches
its fhowy bloffoms; the particles of the duft,
when magnified, appear angular, but become
round when wetted with water. This is not
an uncommon effect of moifture on the duft of

plants

plants. You are well acquainted with the foreign Balfams*, raifed by the gardener in pots,
to adorn the court yard. The genus is charac-
terifed by a calyx of two leaves, a five-petalled
corolla, the bottom of which is received into the
honey-cup of one leaf, fhaped like a hood, and
a capfule of five valves. There is one wild fpecies found chiefly in the northern counties,
which has egg-fhaped leaves, and fruit-ftalks fupporting feveral yellow bloffoms, the ftem fwelling
at the joints; the vulgar name, Touch Me Not,
is expreffive of the elafticity of the capfule,
which, when the feeds are ripe, fuddenly burfts
open witn confiderable force, upon the flighteft
impulfe.

Rejoice with me, that I have at laft reached
the conclufion of this very long letter, and believe, that I fhall ever remain, with undiminifhed
affection, your

FELICIA.

* Impatiens.

LETTER

LETTER XXIV.

DEAR CONSTANCE,   *Shrubbery, Auguſt* 10.

THE twentieth claſs, Gynandria, is diſtinguiſhed from all others, by the circumſtance of
having the ſtamens fixed upon the ſhaft of the
pointal itſelf, or upon a receptacle lengthened
out into the form of a ſhaft ; whereas, we have
hitherto obſerved, that theſe parts have been
perfeĉtly ſeparate and independent of each other.
The orders are marked by the number of ſtamens in each flower. The firſt, called Diandria, from having always two ſtamens, contains
a natural tribe ſo nearly allied, that the form of
the neĉtary alone affords a diſtinĉtion to the ſeveral genera. The ſtruĉture of theſe flowers is
very ſingular, as well as that of the root, each
claims your particular attention. In ſome ſpecies the root is compoſed of a pair of ſolid bulbs;
in others it conſiſts of a ſet of oblong, fleſhy ſub-
ſtances, tapering towards the ends, like the fin-
gers of the hand. The unuſual ſituation of the
parts of fruĉtification in the plants of this family
gives the bloſſoms a very peculiar appearance,
and renders an accurate deſcription of them neceſſary. The oblong ſeed-bud is always placed
below

below the flower, twifted like a fcrew, a fpathe
or fheath fupplies the want of a proper calyx;
the corolla has five petals irregularly fhaped, the
two innermoft uniting over the others in the
form of an arch; the nectary forms the lower
lip, and ftands in the place of the pointal and a
fixth petal; to the inner edge of the nectary adheres the fhaft, which, with its ftigma, is fcarcely
diftinguifhable: the ftamens are very fhort, and
are alfo fixed to the inner rim of the honey cup;
the tips have no covering, their texture refembles the pulp of oranges; two fmall cells, opening downwards, inclofe them, and almoft conceal
them from obfervation. The fpiral germ is
converted into a capfule of three valves, opening at the angles under the keel-fhaped ribs;
within is one cell, containing many feeds like
faw-duft, growing upon a narrow receptacle upon
each valve. The moft numerous genus of this
order is the Orchis, known from the reft by its
horn-fhaped honey-cup; the form of the roots
throws it into three divifions; among thofe with
double bulbs is the Butterfly Orchis, perhaps fo
called from its expanding petals; the horn is
very long, and the lip fpear-fhaped; its greenifh
white bloffoms emit an agreeable fcent, efpecially in the evening. The Purple, late-flowering
Orchis is found in dry paftures, the lip has two
horns, cloven into three clefts, equal and entire;

it

it grows about a foot high, with five or fix fpear-
fhaped leaves proceeding from the root. There
are two kinds very common, called Male and
Female Orchis, but without any reafon for that
diftinction; the Male differs from the Female
by the outer petals being longer and fharper,
and the middle lobe of the cup cloven, and
longer than thofe of the fides; it produces more
flowers, and the ftem is twice as tall. The bloffoms of the Female are white, or red mottled
with white, or violet-coloured; thofe of the
Male are of a deep purple. The broad-leafed
and the fpotted Orchis grow moftly in moift
meadows, the roots of both are palmated or
hand fhaped, though that of the fpotted is more
expanding; the firft has a hollow ftem, and
leaves a little fpotted, but the ftem of the latter
is folid, and the leaves covered with black fpots:
the broad-leafed has a conical honey-cup, and
the lip divided into three lobes, the fide ones reflecting back; the horn in the other fpecies is
fhorter than the germ, and the lip is flat. The
general characters already given of the order will
fuit the next genus, Satyrion *, except particular-
ifing the fhape of the nectary, which terminates
in a bag like a double purfe. The root of the
Lizard flower confifts of two undivided bulbs;
the leaves are fpear-fhaped, and the lip of the

* Satirium.

corolla

corolla cut into three fegments, the middle one
extremely long, and looks as if it had been
bitten off at the end; the bloffoms are white,
inclined to a greenifh hue on the outfide, but
within of a dufky purple; by age the whole co‑
rolla changes to a dingy red: this plant fome‑
times attains the height of three feet. The
Twayblades * form another genus, of which the
honey‑cup is longer than the petals; it hangs
down, and is keeled on the back part. It is
this keel that, in fome fpecies, bears fo clofe a
refemblance to particular infects, as almoft to
deceive the eye at a diftance. Common Tway‑
blade has a fibrous root, and a ftem with only two
leaves, which are egg‑fhaped. The lip is bifect‑
ed. The ftem of Triple Ladies Traces is fome‑
what leafy, the flowers grow fpirally, and all
point one way; the lip is not divided, but only
notched with a fmall fcollop, the three outer
petals are glued together; it flourifhes in barren
paftures, and feldom rifes to a greater height
than five or fix inches. The curious kinds of
Fly and Bee Orchifes, concur in double round‑
ifh bulbs and a ftem furnifhed with leaves. The
Fly Orchis has the lip of the honey‑cup cloven
into four clefts, the wings and helmet are green‑
ifh. The lip of the Bee is divided into five
lobes, bent downwards; the outermoft petals are

* Ophrys.

3   large

large and fpreading, of a purple colour, the two
innermoft green, the lower lip of the honey-cup
is cut into three fegments, and is fhorter than
the petals; the colour is brownifh purple, mixed
with yellow, the upper lip is the longeft, nar-
rowing to a point, and is green; the filaments
are long, and the anthers very large; the feed-
bud exceeds the petals in length, but does not
equal that of the floral leaves. Search for thefe
admirable deceptions among the grafs in chalky
foils; their beauty will amply repay your trouble. Lady's Slipper *, fo named from the fhape
of the nectary, which is fancied to refemble the
form of a flipper, has fibrous roots, the ftem rifes
about a foot high, and is leafy; the leaves are
between egg and fpear-fhape, the purple petals
are fet off to advantage by the pale yellow
honey-cups. The Cuckow Pint †, which we have
frequently gathered under the vulgar name of
Lords and Ladies, is found in hedges, where, in
fpring, it makes its firft appearance by a very
large oblong leaf, in the centre of which is a
club-fhaped fruit-ftalk or receptacle, naked on
the upper part, but covered with feed-buds at
bottom, and with anthers in the middle, fo that
the filaments are unneceffary: as the plant approaches to maturity, the fheath opens and un-
veils the club, which varies gradually, from a

* Cypripedium.   † Arum.

H   yellowifh

yellowifh green, to a fine red purple ; when this
withers, it is fucceeded by a head of round, red
berries, which are acria and poignant, as is the
whole plant.   This extraordinary genus has per-
plexed botanifts where to place it.

The unufual figure, as well as beauty, of many
of the plants defcribed in this letter, will furely
ferve you for entertainment, till I have leifure to
write again : in the interim, be affured of my entire affeftion.

FELICIA.

LETTER XXV.

DEAR CONSTANCE,   *Shrubbery, Auguft* 13.

THE twenty-firft clafs, Monoecia, which now
falls under confideration, differs, in a very effential particular, from any yet obferved ; we are no
longer to look for perfeft flowers within the
fame empalement, but may expeft to find the
bloffoms of an individual plant varying in charafter, fome bearing ftamens only, and others
pointals alone.   The former are barren, yielding
no

no feed, but the piftilliferous flowers produce a
germ, furnifhed with feeds.   Ditches, ponds,
and ftagnant waters nourifh moft of the Stone-
worts * ; the fertile bloffoms have a cup of four
awl-fhaped leaves, the two outer ones longeft
and oppofite, the corolla is wanting, the feed-
bud fhaped like a turban, and produces one folitary, egg-fhaped feed; the barren flowers grow
at the bafe of the feed-bud, on the outfide of
the empalement.   There are feveral fpecies, but
as you cannot gather them without wetting your
feet, it will be needlefs to fpecify their minute
diftinctions.   The very numerous tribe of
Sedges †, having three ftamens, belongs to the
third order, and generally grows in bogs and
marfhy places : both kinds of flowers are borne
on catkins, confifting of fcales, each containing
a fingle flower, neither kind has any corolla ;
the fertile flowers have a three-toothed nectary,
which is puffed up, and within which is the triangular feed-bud, a very fhort fhaft with three
ftigmas; and laftly, a three cornered feed.   Some
of thefe have but one fpike, others have many,
compofed of fertile and barren flowers promif-
cuoufly; but they are more ufually found on
diftinct fpikes.   In the latter divifion is one
fpecies, of which the upright fpikes grow together by threes, the barren one terminating,

* Chara.   † Carex.
H 2   and

and the two lower fertile ones being almoſt
black ; a little leaf, longer than the ſpike, grows
beneath the lower one, the bright green leaves
are long and narrow, and the ſtem is a naked
ſtraw with three equal flat ſides; by means of
this plant, boggy moſſes are converted into firm
uſeful land.   The Burreed * and the Reedmace † have a near affinity to each other.   In
the firſt, the flowers of both kinds grow in a
roundiſh head ; the barren ones above, and thoſe
with pointals beneath ; each has a ſimilar empalement, conſiſting of three leaves, the ſummits
are two, and the ſeed is as hard as bone.   Neither of theſe plants has any corolla ; the catkin,
in the Reedmace, is formed like a cylinder, cloſe
ſet with flowers of both kinds, arranged in the
ſame order as thoſe of the Burreed ; the cup of
the ſtameniferous flowers has three briſtle-ſhaped
leaves, but that of the piſtilliferous ones, only
feathered hairs, and a ſingle ſeed ſupported in a
kind of briſtle.   The greater Burreed has upright, three-cornered leaves, but thoſe of the
ſmaller kind are drooping and flat ; the Great
Catſtail, or Reedmace, reaches to the height of
ſix feet ; the leaves are very long and narrow,
and ſword-ſhaped ; the two ſpikes grow near together ; but in the leſſer kind, they are more diſ-
tant, and the leaves are ſemicylindrical.   In the

* Sparganium.   † Typha.

fourth

fourth order, Tetrandria, you will find Roman
Nettle* ; the ftameniferous flowers have a cup of
four leaves; inftead of the petals, a honey-cup is
placed in the centre of the flowers : the piftilliferous flowers are not always on the fame plant,
but are fometimes feen on diftant ones ; they
have a cup formed of two valves, which clofing,
fupplies the place of a feed-veffel ; they have no
corolla. The difagreeable effect of the ftings
you have doubtlefs felt ; let them make you
amends, by amufing you in the microfcope ; in
fhape, they refemble the ftings of infects, long
tapering, and finely pointed. Notwithftanding
their minutenefs, they are hollow, and convey a
poifonous fluid, which lurks in a fmall bag at
the bafe of the fting : upon the fting meeting
with refiftance, it preffes upon this little bag,
and acts like a fyringe. Both kinds of flowers
proceed in bunches together, from the buds of
the Box Tree †, thofe which are barren, have a
cup of three leaves, a corolla of two petals, and
the rudiment of a feed-bud, without either fhaft
or fummit ; the fertile flowers have a four-leav-
ed calyx, a three-petalled corolla, three pointals,
and a three-celled capfule, with three bills, opening as a fpring three ways, each cell containing
two feeds ; the bloffoms are greenifh, and the
leaves oval, thick, and gloffy, and, by their dura-

* Urtica.   † Buxus.

H 3   tion

tion through the winter, contribute to the beauty
of plantations and pleafure-grounds in that dreary
feafon.   There are many varieties, but they all
belong to one fpecies. The Birch * produces
each kind of flowers in feparate catkins, which
are compofed of fcales; thofe which are ftameniferous have three flowers in each fcale, the
flowers confift of three equal florets, with four
fmall clefts.   The. piftilliferous catkins have
only two flowers in each fcale, without any perceptible corolla; but thefe are fucceeded by feeds
bordered by a membrane. The Alder is of the
fame genus, and differs from the common Birch
in its branched fruit-ftalks, and round clammy
notched leaves; whereas, thofe of the Birch are
egg-fhaped, tapering to a point, and the bark is
white, fmooth, and gloffy. Several ftately trees
are included in the eight order, Polyandria; the
Oak, the Beech, the Hazle, and the Hornbeam.
The Oak †, fo valuable for its timber, and the
various ufeful purpofes to which its different
parts are applied, claims precedency.   The barren flowers hang upon a loofe catkin, their calyx
is of one leaf, bloffom they have none; the number of the ftamens is from five to ten; the calyx
of the fertile flowers, which are feated in a bud,
is like leather, and confifts of one leaf; they have
one pointal fplit into five parts, the feed is an

* Betula.   † Quercus.

oval

oval nut, called an acorn, covered with a tough
shell, and fixed into the cup. The barren
flowers of the Beech* are fixed to a common
receptacle, somewhat like a catkin; they have a
bell-shaped calyx of one leaf, but divided into
five clefts; the stamens are about twelve: the
fertile flowers grow from buds on the same tree,
and have a calyx with four teeth and three pointals; the calyx becomes a capsule beset with soft
thorns, containing two nuts. The Chesnut is a
species of the Beech, distinguished by spear-
shaped leaves, a little notched at the edges, and
smooth underneath. But the Common Beech
has egg-shaped leaves, indistinctly notched, and
a smooth, white bark, the barren catkins round
like a ball. As in several preceding genera, the
barren flowers in the Hazel † are formed on a
long cylindrical catkin, and the fertile ones at a
distance from the others, sitting inclosed in a
bud on the same shrub; for the Hazel, Filbert,
&c. do not rank with trees; the scales of the
catkins bend inwards, with three clefts, each scale
containing a single flower, furnished generally
with-eight stamens; the calyx of the fertile
flowers has two upright leaves, jagged at the
edge, each flower has two very long, red shafts,
with simple summits: the fruit is a nut, to which
you are no stranger; neither sort of flowers

* Fagus.   † Corylus.

H 4   has

has any corolla; the leaves of the Common
Hazle are oval, pointed, toothed, and wrinkled ;
the catkins are green at firſt, but change to
brown. In the Hornbeam *, the different forts
of flowers are produced in feparate catkins ; both
have a fingle flower in each fcale : the number
of ſtamens varies, but is generally about ten ; the
fertile flowers have two germs, each bearing two
pointals ; the catkins growing very large, inclofe the feed at the bafe of the fcales ; the
leaves are wrinkled, oval, and pointed, and
ſharply indented at the edges. In the order,
Monadelphia, I ſhall remark only the Fir †, belonging to a natural family, called Lone-bearing
Trees. The barren flowers are produced in
bunches, and have many ſtamens united below
into an upright pillar, but feparated at the top ;
the fertile flowers grow on a cone, two of them
in each fcale ; they have no corolla, one pointal,
and a nut enlarged by a membranaceous wing.
In the broad-leaved trees, where the ſtamens
and pointals are produced in feparate empale-
ments, either on the fame, or on diſtinct trees,
the flowers come out before the leaves are fully
expanded, that the leaves might not intercept
the duſt of the anthers in its paſſage to the pointals, by which they are fertilized; but nature
ever an œconomiſt, makes no fuch arrangement

* Carpinus.   † Pinus.

among

among thofe trees which have narrow leaves;
fuch as the Fir or Yew. This is a remarkable
inftance of defign, and clearly proves that all
parts of creation, if properly obferved, would
furnifh us with examples of the wifdom of an
infinite wife Creator, who not only formed every
thing in the beginning, but has provided, in a
wonderful manner, for their prefervation and increafe. With this ferious reflection I fhall conclude, wifhing you all kinds of happinefs.

FELICIA.

L E T T E R XXVI.

DEAR CONSTANCE, *Shrubbery, Auguft* 17.

THE only diftinction between the laft clafs
we have examined, and the twenty-fecond, which
we are going to inveftigate, confifts in the difpofition of the refpective kinds of flowers. In the
former clafs, both kinds were produced on the
fame plant; but in this, Dioecia, they muft be
fought for on different plants of the fame fpecies. This will coft you fome trouble, but we

H 5   may

may remember my mother's favourite maxim,
that nothing is to be obtained without its proportion of labour. The Willow * belongs to
the fecond order ; the number of ftamens is not
always the fame in the different fpecies ; in fome
there are three or five, of unequal length, and
one kind produces complete flowers within the
fame empalement. Two is the number that diftinguifhes the order, and which generally prevails ; the genus contains many fpecies, that concur in the following charaſters : each kind of
flower grows on a fcaled catkin, with a fingle
flower in each fcale, which has no corolla ; the
barren flowers have a very fmall cylindrical,
honied gland, placed in their centre ; in thofe
which are fertile is an egg-fhaped feed-bud, tapering into a fhaft, hardly diftinſt from the
germ, and terminating in two cloven, upright
fummits ; the capfule has one cell and two
valves, and inclofes many fmall feeds, crowned
with a fimple, hairy feather. The Common
Willow being familiar to you, I fhall pafs it by,
and feleſt the Round-leaved Willow for its fingularity ; moſt of the tribe flourifh in moiſt, watery fituations ; but this fpecies is found on
mountains. Its leaves are fmooth, entire, and
egg-fhaped, their upper furface is green and
wrinkled, the under one is bluifh, and covered

Salix.

with

with a network of veins, which are at firſt red,
but afterwards become green. It is but a low
ſhrub, and produces both flowers and leaves from
the ſame bud. The fourth order preſents you
with the Miſletoe * ; the ſtameniferous flowers
have a cup with four diviſions, to each one of
which is fixed an anther without a filament; the
piſtilliferous flowers moſtly grow oppoſite to the
others, their cup conſiſts of four leaves, ſitting
on the germ, they have no ſtyle, and the feed-
veſſel is a globular one, called berry, containing
a ſingle, heart-ſhaped feed; neither kind of
flower has any corolla. The ſeeds of this plant
are ſuppoſed to be propagated by birds, which
ſwallow them whole, and drop them on the
branches of trees, where they vegetate, by infi-
nuating the fibrous parts of their roots into the
woody ſubſtance of the tree. The White Miſletoe is found upon Willows, Oaks, Hazels, Apple, and Pear Trees, but moſt frequently upon
Crab Trees. It has ſpear-ſhaped, blunt leaves;
a forked ſtem, the flowers are produced in ſpikes
in the boſom of the leaves, the bloſſoms have a
greeniſh hue, and the berries are white. The
Hop † will afford us a ſpecimen of the fifth order: the barren flowers have a cup of five
leaves; in the fertile ones, it is one-leafed, expanding in an oblique manner, and entire; each

* Viſcum.   † Humulus.

H 6

of thefe is furnifhed with two pointals and one
feed, and the whole is inclofed within a leafy calyx ; neither kind has any corolla : what is generally called a Hop is only a clufter of many of thefe
flowers. The only fpecies known has toothed
leaves, divided into lobes and climbing ftems.
The Poplar * is comprifed in the eighth order :
both kinds of flowers grow on oblong catkins,
confifting of fcales, each fcale inclofing a fingle
flower, and ragged at the edge ; neither has any
petals ; both have a turban-fhaped nectary, ending obliquely at the top in an egg-fhaped border;
the fertile flowers have fcarcely any fhaft, but the
fummit is divided into four clefts ; the feed-
veffel is a capfule of two cells, containing many
feathered feeds. The Great White Poplar, or
Abele Tree, has circular leaves, cut angularly at
the edges, and downy underneath. The leaves
of the Trembling Poplar, or Afpen Tree, refemble thofe of the laft-mentioned kind, except in
having fmooth furfaces on both fides ; the leaf-
ftalks are long and flattened towards the ends,
which caufes the leaves to fhake and vibrate with
the fmalleft breeze. In flow ftreams and wet
ditches is found Frogbit †, which belongs to the
ninth order : the barren flowers have a cup of
three leaves, and a corolla of three petals, and
grow by threes in a fheath of two oblong leaves ;

* Populus.   † Hydrocharis.

the

the nine ſtamens are in three rows, from the middlemoſt proceeds an awl-ſhaped, little pillar, reſembling a ſhaft; the other two rows are unit-ed at the baſe, and there is the rudiment of a ſeed-bud in the centre of the flower. Thoſe that are fertile grow ſolitarily, the cup and co-rolla are ſimilar to the ſame parts in the barren flowers; the ſeed-bud is beneath; there are ſix pointals, and the capſule reſembles leather, with ſix cells filled with many ſmall, roundiſh ſeeds. There is but one known ſpecies which has ſmooth, thick, kidney-ſhaped leaves and white bloſſoms. In the order Monadelphia, is the Juniper *, the barren flowers are borne upon a conical catkin, the ſcales of which ſerve the purpoſe of a calyx; they have three ſtamens but no corolla; in the fertile flowers, the calyx is permanent, and has three diviſions growing to the ſeed-bud, which is beneath; the corolla con-ſiſts of three petals, the pointals are three, the ſeed-veſſel is a berry containing three ſeeds, and marked in the lower part with three oppoſite tu-bercles, which were formerly the cup, and at the top by three little teeth, which were originally the petals. In the common kind, the ſharp-pointed leaves grow by threes, longer than the berry, expanding; it will thrive in almoſt any ſoil, but, in ſome ſituations, dwindles to a mere

* Juniperus.

ſhrub.

fhrub. The melancholy Yew *, placed in
church-yards, to give additional folemnity to
thofe repofitories of the dead, has neither bloffom nor empalement, unlefs we chufe to call the
bud by that name, which confifts of three or
four leaves; the ftamens are numerous, terminated by anthers with eight clefts: the fertile
flowers have an egg-fhaped germ, ending in a
blunt ftigma without any fhaft, which is changed
to a fingular kind of berry, or rather fucculent
receptacle, open at the end, and of a red colour,
having one oblong feed ftanding out of the open
end: the leaves of the common kind grow clofe
together, in a double row along the ftem, like
the back bone of fome fifh, and, when frefh, are a
fatal poifon. The Pettigree † is of the fourteenth
order, Syngenefia, in which the calyx, bloffom, and
honey-cup are the fame in both kinds of flowers;
the firft has fix. leaves. bloffom there is none,
but an egg-fhaped, puffed up honey-cup, open
at the rim, grows in the centre of the flower.
The barren flowers have no filaments, but they
have three anthers united together at the bafe,
on the end of the honey cup: the oblong germ,
in the fertile flowers, is concealed within the
honey-cup; they have one pointal and a globular
berry for a feed-veffel, which contains two
round feeds: the fpecies called Butcher's

* Taxus..   † Rufcus.

Broom .

Broom bears its flowers on the upper furface of the leaves, which are like thofe of the Myrtle, except being ftiff and prickly at the points ; the bloffoms are of a yellowifh green, and the berries red. I become every day more impatient for your return, as the time appointed for it approaches. Mrs. Snelgrove intends that we fhall apply very clofely in the winter to drawing, that we may be qualified to delineate the botanical fpecimens we fhall collect the following fummer, that, by combining two branches of our education, we may improve in both at the fame time. Adieu!

FELICIA.

LETTER XXVII.

Shrubbery, Auguft 25.

THE difpofition of the flowers, my dear Conftance, is the circumftance upon which the twenty-third order, Polygamia, depends; its chief characteriftic is, that both complete flowers, and one or both forts of incomplete ones, are either
produced

produced on the fame plant, or on different individuals of the fame fpecies. The firft order
contains thofe plants that always produce flowers
furnifhed with all the parts of fruƐification, as
well as thofe that are deficient in fome of them,
on the fame individual. Two of the graffes are
included in this order; the calyx and coroĦa
of Soft Grafs * are fupplied by chaffy hufks
of two valves, the perfeƐ flowers have three ftamens and two pointals, though they have but
one feed: the barren flowers are fmaller than
the others, and are placed among them; they
likewife have three ftamens, but are without corolla, pointal, or feed. The hufks inclofe each
two florets; thofe which contain the perfeƐ kind
are without awns; but in the creeping fpecies,
the imperfeƐ florets have jointed awns, and the
hufks are fmooth. The hufks are woolly in the
Meadow Soft Grafs, and the barren florets have
crooked awns. In the Hard Grafs † the complete flowers are lateral, and the barren ones
grow between them; all three are inclofed in a
very large hufk of two valves. The ftamens are
three, and the pointals two, in the perfeƐ
flowers: the fame number cf ftamens prevails in
thofe flowers which are imperfeƐ. The flowers
of the Maple ‡ grow in bunches, the perfeƐ
ones towards the lower part, and the barren

* Holcus.   † Ægilops.   ‡ Acer.

ones

ones near the end.   They are fimilar, with re-
fpe&t to the calyx, corolla, and ftamens ; the firft
is divided into five clefts, the fecond confifts of
five petals, and the ftamens are eight in number;
the complete flowers have befides one pointal,
and two roundifh capfules united at the bafe,
each terminating in a large membranaceous
wing, and containing one feed.   The leaves of
the Sycamore, which is one fpecies of this genus, are divided into five lobes, unequally notched, and the flowers hang in large bunches : the
bark of the Common Maple is rough and furrowed, the leaves are cut into blunt lobes, with
fmaller indentures.   In the Pellitory of the
Wall*, the incomplete flowers are furnifhed with
pointals, but are deficient in ftamens ; they are
placed between thofe that are perfe&, within the
fame fence, which is flat and confifts of fix
leaves ; the calyx of both kinds is four cleft,
they have no corolla, one pointal, and one feed.
There are four ftamens in the perfe& flowers.
The common fort is known by lance-fhaped
leaves, forked fruit-ftalks, and cups with two
leaves : the flowers that are imperfe& are four-
edged and pyramidal.   The Afh† belongs to the
fecond order : it frequently happens that the fame
tree produces complete flowers, accompanied by
thofe which are piftilliferous or ftameniferous,

* Parietaria.   † Fraxinus.

but

but the former are generally upon a diſtinct
tree; they have either no calyx, or one with
four clefts; no corolla, or one with four petals:
the pointal is one, and the ſtamens two, in the
complete flowers, with one flat, ſpear-ſhaped
feed; the Common Aſh has winged leaves,
ſlightly notched, the ſide buds ſend forth flowers,
the terminating ones leaves, the piſtilliferous
flowers are without either petals or empalement.

With great affection to all our friends that are
with you, I conclude truly your's,

FELICIA.

L. E T T E R   XXVIII.

Shrubbery, September 10.

WE are at length arrived, my dear Conſtance,
at the laſt claſs, Cryptogamia, which I have already told you, includes thoſe vegetables which
are of the loweſt kinds, whoſe parts of fructification have hitherto eſcaped the moſt attentive re-
ſearches of learned botaniſts, therefore, Mrs.
Snelgrove has recommended only a very few of
the

the moſt obnoxious to my notice, which, ſhe
ſays, may ſerve to give us general ideas of the
reſt. The parts of fruƐtification in the Ferns are
ſometimes produced in ſpikes, but in general
they are found upon the backs of the leaves, and,
when magnified, appear to conſiſt of a ſcale proceeding from the leaf, with an opening on one
ſide; ſome little globules lie concealed beneath
this ſcale, ſupported on foot-ſtalks and ſurrounded by an elaſtic ring; when the ſeed·is ready for
diſperſion, theſe balls burſt, and.there iſſues a fine
powder from them, which is believed to be the
ſeeds. Horſetail *, Adderſtongue †, and Moonwort ‡, have their fruƐtification upon ſpikes;
each ſeparate one belonging to the firſt, is round
and gaping at its baſe, compoſed of many valves.
That ſpecies, which is found in moiſt, corn fields,
bears its fruit upon a naked ſtalk; other leafy
ſtalks, that are barren, come up later, and continue after the firſt are ſhrivelled. The rough,
naked ſtem of the Shave Graſs, is uſed by tur-
ners and cabinet-makers to give their work a
poliſh. The capſules in Adderſtongue point
along both ſides of the ſpike in a jointed row,
which is divided into as many cells as there are
joints; theſe cells, when the ſeeds are ripe, open
croſſways. The common ſpecies is diſtinguiſhed
by an egg-ſhaped leaf, and a very ſlender ſpike

* Equiſetum.　† Ophiogloſſum.　‡ Oſmunda.

growing

growing on a fruit-ftalk. Moonwort has globular capfules difpofed in a bunch ; the feeds are
very fmall and numerous. The common fort
grows in hilly paftures; it has a folitary, naked
ftem, and one winged leaf. The Ofmund
Royal is found in putrid marfhes, its leaves are
doubly winged, and bear bunches of flowers at
the ends. Ruftyback * has the whole under furface of the leaves covered with the fruĉtification.
In the various fpecies of Polypody †, each fructification forms a diftinĉt, round dot, placed on
the under furface of the leaf. There are many
fpecies, generally known by the name of Ferns;
that which occurs moft commonly is called Make
Fern, and is found in woods, heaths, and ftony
places ; it has a chaffy ftem, the leaves are
doubly winged, the wings blunt and a little fcolloped. Spleenwort ‡ produces its fruĉtifications
in ftraight lines. Hartftongue has entire fimple
leaves, refembling the form of a tongue, with
hairy ftalks ; it grows on moift, fhady rocks. In
Maidenhair § the flowers are difpofed in oval
fpots, towards the ends of the leaves, which are
turned back upon them. The true Maidenhair
has leaves which are doubly compound, the little
leaves alternate, the wings are fhaped like a
wedge, divided into lobes, and grow upon foot-
ftalks. Let us now proceed to the Moffes, which

* Acroftichum. † Polypodium. ‡ Afplenium. § Adiantum.

diffen

differ from the Ferns, in having leaves diftinct
from the ftalk; from the midft of thefe leaves
are feen fmall threads, terminated by a fmall
body, the whole correfponding with ftamens;
fhorter threads, fuppofed to be pointals, fometimes grow on the fame plant, and fometimes
upon a diftinct one; the tips of the longer
threads have been difcovered to be capfules: in
fome genera, they are covered with a veil or cap;
in others, they are without this defence; which
diftinction ferves as a divifion to the order.
Moffes, though apparently infignificant, are not
ufelefs; they protect the roots of tender plants
equally from the extremes of cold and heat; and
many kinds of them, by vegetating in the fhallow parts of pools and marfhes, convert, in the
courfe of a long period of time, that fpace,
which before was only water and bog, into ufeful land and fruitful paftures. Neither Club-
mofs *, Bogmofs †, or Earthmofs ‡ has any veil;
the firft has a two-valved capfule, fitting at the
bafe of the leaves; the fecond has a fmooth
mouth, and the capfule covered with a lid; and
the third is known by its fringed mouth, covered
with a lid tapering to a point. Hairmofs § has
a capfule covered with a conical lid, fitting upon
a fmall rifing eminence, which fupplies the place
of a receptacle, a woolly veil protects this cap-

* Lycopodium.   † Sphagnum.   ‡ Phafcum.   § Polytrichum.

3   fule;

fule ; the fertile flower is fuppofed to grow on a
diftinct individual, under the form of a little
rofe or ftar. The Great Golden Maidenhair, the
commoneft fpecies of this genus, has a fimple
ftem, and the capfule is of a long, fquare fhape.
Marfhmofs *, like Hairmofs, has two kinds of
fructification ; the one a capfule with a lid, covered with a fmooth veil; the other compofed of
leaves, arranged in the form of a ftar or rofe,
with many dufty, globular particles collected into
a ball in the centre.   None of thefe fertile
flowers, as they are imagined to be, are found in
either Threadmofs † or Feathermofs ‡, but they
both have a lidded capfule, covered with a fmooth
veil.   Bryum, or Threadmofs, is diftinguifhed
by a naked ftalk, and a tubercle at the bafe of
it ; whereas the fruit-ftalks, in the Hypnum or
Feathermofs, rife from the fides of the fhoots,
and their bafe is furrounded by a fcaly bulb.
There is one fpecies of Threadmofs that is a
great prefervative to thatch ; it has nearly upright lips and reflected leaves, which terminate
in hoary hairs; happy is it for the cottager,
when this mofs takes to vegetate on the roof of
his humble dwelling ; it forms a defence againft
the injuries of weather, that will laft for many
years.   The Fern Feathermofs is diminutive,
but extremely elegant; it grows in fhady places

* Mnium.   † Bryum.   ‡ Hypnum.

or

or upon the banks of ditches; the fruit-ftalks
rife from the end. The wings are fimple,
though winged; the tips are crefted with a lid
of a lively red, and the mouth edged with a
fringe of the fame colour. The Sea Weeds and
Liverworts are included in the third order;
fome people call them Thongs, becaufe the fubftance of many of them refembles leather; the
parts of their fructification are too little known,
to fupply a regular account of them; for they
fcarcely admit of a diftinction of root, leaf, or
ftem; much lefs can we form a precife idea of
the more minute parts of the flower; there are
fmall bodies perceptible in the Liverworts, which
are conjectured to be the refpective kinds of
flowers, diftinct from each other; the fruit and
flowers in the Sea Weeds are fuppofed to confift of little bladders, fome of which are hollow,
and contain hairs within them; others are filled
with a kind of jelly. As thefe matters are not
yet fufficiently afcertained, to produce a certain-
ty, we muft wait patiently till further experiments of naturalifts throw more light upon the
fubject. Many of thefe are ufeful in commenc-
ing the operations of nature, in the growth of
vegetables upon the bareft rocks, receiving no
other fupport than what the air and rains afford
them; as they decay, they are converted into a
very fine mould, which nourifhes other fpecies;

thefe,

thefe, in their turn, are changed into food for
Moffes, &c. and they likewife rot, and, in length
of time, a foil is formed from the refufe of the
whole, capable of maintaining trees, plants, &c.
The Lichens, or Liverworts, fpread themfelves
like meal, cruft, leaf, or thread over the ground,
rocks, plants, or trees; and, being very numerous, are fubdivided, according to the various peculiarities of the receptacle and manner of
growth; this genus has a roundifh, flat, fhining,
gummy receptacle, and the leaves are covered
with a meal or duft. The firft feétion is tuber-
cled; they adhere clofely to the bark of trees, in
the form of a cruft, ftudded with convex recep-
tacles or tubercles, which are frequently thought
to refemble the lines in writing or maps. The
fecond is the faucer-like, becaufe the cruft is
fprinkled with hollow receptacles, fomewhat like
faucers. Thirdly, the tiled, are compofed of
many fmall leaves growing circularly, the fmalleft in the middle, and thofe which are largeft on
the outfrde. Fourthly, the leafy is diftinguifhed
by leaves that are detached from the fubftance
upon which they grow, and are jagged or torn in
various direétions. The faucers, or fhields, are
large, and frequently grow on fruit-ftalks, either
in the divifions of the leaves, or upon their edges.
There is one fpecies that is rather upright and
leafy, it is white and downy underneath, and
branched

branched like the horns of a ſtag, which has an extraordinary capacity of imbibing and retaining odours, and on that account is uſeful to the perfumers, as a baſis for ſcented powders. Fifthly, Leatherlike : the leaves of this diviſion reſemble leather in ſubſtance ; the ſhields, which are large, are moſtly found upon the edges of the leaves. Sixthly, Sooty, appearing black as if burnt, and adhering only in one point to the ſubſtance upon which they grow. Seventhly, Cup-bearing, conſiſting at firſt of a granulous cruſt, which afterwards unfolds into ſmall leaves; from theſe ariſes a ſtem, ſupporting the receptacles, which are formed like a cup or drinking-glaſs; upon the edges of theſe cups are frequently ſeen little brown or ſcarlet tubercles. Eightly, Shrubby, branching out like ſhrubs or coral. The celebrated Rein Deer Moſs belongs to this diviſion : it is perforated, much branched, the ſmaller branches nodding. This is almoſt the only vegetable to be found in the inhoſpitable climate of Lapland, during the dreary ſeaſon of winter ; but it makes amends for the want of others, by ſupporting the Rein Deer, an animal, which not only affords food to the Laplander, but ſupplies him with every neceſſary of life. Ninthly, Threadlike : the branches ſhooting out like ſo many threads, moſtly from the branches of trees, which gives this kind the name of Treemoſs. It is high time

I   to

to proceed to the Sea Weeds, which are comprifed in the three following genera, Laver * :
Oarweed †, and Riverweed ‡. The fubftance of
the firft of thefe plants is membranaceous, and
the parts of the fructification are inclofed in a
membrane, rather tranfparent and like a bladder.
The Oarweed, Sea-weed, or Sea-wrack, as it is
fometimes called, is leathery, and has two kinds
of bladders, one of which is fmooth and hollow,
and interwoven with hairs, and is efteemed to be
the barren flowers; the others, regarded as the
fertile flowers, are filled with a kind of jelly,
which contains fmall perforated grains, in each
of which is a folitary feed. The Riverweeds
are compofed of unequal tubercles, growing on
very long hair-like fibres. We are not likely to
examine many of the two laft genera, unlefs we
fhall be able to perfuade my mother to make an
excurfion to the fea fide, as moft of them are
found on the fea fhore, or in rivers and flow
ftreams. There remains now only the Mufh-
rooms, or Fungi, to fpeak of, which you know at
firft fight, from the fingularity of their appearance, being deftitute of either branches, leaves,
flowers, or any thing fimilar to the parts of fructification in other vegetables. The Mufhroom §,
a very extenfive genus, grows horizontally, and
is furnifhed with gills on the under furface;

* Ulva. † Fucus. ‡ Conferva. § Agaricus.

3   that

that fpecies, of it which is common at the tables
of the opulent, and valued for its high flavour,
has a convex, fcaly white head, which is fupported on a ftalk or pillar, and the gills are red; it
grows in woods or parks, where the land has
been long unploughed. The Spunk * is another genus which grows horizontally, but differs from the laft, in having pores inftead of gills
on the under furface. The Morell † is known
by a fmooth furface underneath, and a kind of
network on the upper part. That which is eaten
has a naked, wrinkled pillar, and a hat that is
egg-fhaped and full of cells. Puffball ‡ is a
Fungus of a roundifh form, and filled with a
mealy powder, fuppofed to be the feeds. The
Truffle ufed for food has no root, but grows
beneath the furface of the ground; it is round
and folid, the outfide is rough. The method of
finding, this fubterraneous delicacy, is by dogs,
which are taught to hunt for it by fcent; as foon
as they perceive it, they begin to bark and
fcratch up the ground, a fure indication to their
employers, that the treafure they are in fearch
of is at hand. The propenfities and inftinéts of
animals, is an inexhauftible fource of wonders
to thofe who are acquainted with them. The
ftruéture of plants has furnifhed us with much
fubjeét of admiration, from the flight furvey only

* Boletus. † Phallus. ‡ Hycoperdon.

that

that we have taken of them, which furely fhould excite us to obferve them with further attention, as leifure and opportunity offer.

Thus, my dear fifter, I have gone through all the claffes, fuperficially indeed, but perhaps fufficiently diffufe, to give you a tafte for my favourite purfuit, which is every thing I had in view when I began this correfpondence, to which your return next week will put an agreeable termination; I fhall rejoice to refign my office of inftructrefs to my dear Mrs. Snelgrove, who unites with my mother and me, in impatiently wifhing for the day, that fhall reftore beloved Conftance to her affectionate

FELICIA.

PLATE

Fig. 1

Fig. 4

Fig. 3

Fig. 2

Fig. 5

Fig. 6

Fig. 7

Fig. 8

Fig. 9

Fig. 10

Fig. 11

Fig. 12

Fig. 13

Fig. 14

Fig. 15

PLATE I.

E̲MPALEMENTS, or Parts of Flowers, Letter 3.

———

PLATE II.

Fig. 1.   Calyx or Cup, as in the Polyanthus.

Fig. 2.   Involucrum; a Fence or Univerſal Umbel; *a*, general; *b*, partial.

Fig. 3.   Amentum or Catkin.

Fig. 4.   A Spatha or Sheath.

Fig. 5.   A Glume, Calyx, or Huſk; *c c* the Valves; *d d*, the Awns.

Fig. 6.   A Veil, as in *Moſſes*; *a*, Capitulum or Head; *b*, the Operculum or Lid; *c*, Calyptre, Hood or Extinguiſher.

Fig. 7.   A Cap, as in *Muſhrooms*; *a*, Cap or Hat; *b*, Valve; *c*, Stipe of a *Fungus*.

Fig. 8.   *a*, The Receptacle of a compound Flower, not Chaffy.

Fig. 9.   A Spatha and Spadix.

Fig. 10.   Strobilus, a Cone; a Pericarpium formed from an Amentum or Catkin, as Fig. 3.

Fig. 11.   *a*, The Pollen viewed with a Microſcope; *b*, an elaſtic Vapour diſcharged from it.

HONEY-CUPS.

Fig. 12.   A Bell-ſhaped Honey-cup which crowns the Corolla, as in the *Narciſſus*; *a*, the Cup or Nectarium.

I 3   Fig.

Fig. 13. Nectaries in the *Parnaffus;* thirteen between each Stamen.

Fig. 14. The horned Honey-cups of the Aconite.

Fig. 15. The Scale or Honey-cup at the bottom of a Petal of the Crown Imperial.

—H—

PLATE III.

BLOSSOMS.

Fig. 1. A Bell-fhaped Bloffom.
Fig. 2. A Funnel-fhaped Bleffom.
Fig. 3. A Ringent Bloffom.
Fig. 4. A Perfonate Bloffom.
Fig. 5. A Cruciform Bloffom.
Fig. 6. A Butterfly-fhaped Bloffom.
Fig. 7. A Compound Radiate Flower.

FOLIATION.

By this term we underftand the ftate the Leaves are in, whilft they remain concealed within the *Buds* of the Plant. Linnæus claims the difcovery of thefe diftinctions, preceding Botanifts not having attended to the *complicate,* or folded ftate of the Leaves, which are in their manner, either, a,

Fig. 8. Convolute, *rolled together;* when the margin of one fide furrounds the other margin of the fame Leaf, in the manner of a Cowl or Hood, as in Indian Flowering Reed, Saxifrage, and many Graffes.

Fig. 9. Involute, *rolled in;* when their lateral margins are rolled fpirally inwards, as in the Poplar, Pear, Violet, &c. &c.

PLATE. III.

Fig. 10. Revolute, *rolled back*; when their lateral
margins are rolled fpirally backwards, as in Rofe-
mary, Foxglove, Coltsfoot, &c. &c.

Fig. 11. Conduplicate, *doubled together*; when the
fides of the Leaf are parallel and approach each
other, as in Oak, Beech, Walnut, &c. &c.

Fig. 12. Equitant, *riding*; when the fides of the
Leaves lie parallel, and approach in fuch a manner,
as the outer embrace the inner, as in Flower de
Luce, Sweet Rufh, and fome Graffes.

Fig. 13. *Imbricated*; when the Leaves are *parallel*
with a ftraight furface, and lie one over the other,
as in Lilac, Privet, Croffwort, &c.

Fig. 14. Obvolute, *rolled againft* each other; when
their refpective margins alternately embrace the
ftraight margin of the oppofite Leaf, as in the Pink,
Campion, Valerian, &c.

Fig. 15. Plaited; when their complication is in
plaits lengthways, like plicate Leaves, as in the
Maple, Marfh Mallow, Vine, &c.

Fig. 16. Convolute, fee Fig. 8; more than one Leaf
convoluted.

Fig. 17. Involute, oppofite. } See Involute.
Fig. 18. Involute, alternate.

Fig. 19. Revolute, oppofite. See Fig. 10.

Fig. 20. Equitant, two edged; Equitant, two pro-
minent Angles. See the difference in Fig. 12,
which has not thofe Angles.

Fig. 21. Equitant, three fided; Equitant, three
ways, fo as to form a triangle.

PLATE

PLATE IV.

CLASSES, to face Letter VII.

———

PLATE V.

SEED-VESSELS.

Fig. 1. The Capsule of a *Poppy* ; *m*, the radiate summit ; *n*, the hole through which the feeds escape.

Fig. 2. A Shell or Legumen, in which the feeds are fixed to the upper seam only.

Fig. 3. A Pod or Siliqua, in which the feeds are fixed to the seam alternately.

Fig. 4. A Berry (Bacca) cut across, to show the feeds.

Fig. 5. A Flefhy Capsule or Pear ; *a*, the Pome or Pulp ; *b*, the Capfule included ; *c*, one of the Seeds raised.

Fig. 6. A Pulpy Seed-vefsel ; Drupa or Stone-fruit ; *a*, the Pulp or Drupa ; *b*, the Nucleus or Stone.

Fig. 7. A Capsule gaping at top.

Fig. 8. A Capsule longitudinally diffected, that the Receptacle of the Seeds may appear.

Fig. 9. Of the Parts of a Capfule ; *a*, the Valvalet ; *b*, the Partition ; *c*, the Column or Pillar ; *d*, Receptacle.

Fig. 10. A winged Seed ; *o*, the hairy Pappus ; *p*, the Feathery Pappus ; *q*, Seed ; *r*, Stipe of the Pappus.

Fig. 11. A Folliculus or little bag ; *f*, a Receptacle of Seeds.

z   PLATE

PLATE. V.

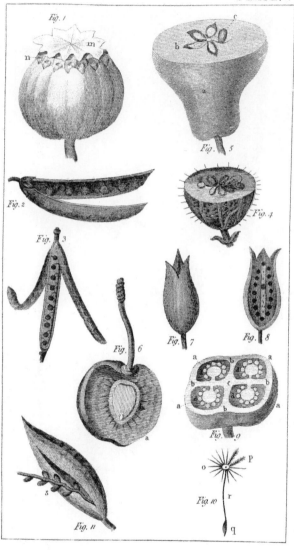

Fig. 1

Fig. 5

Fig. 2

Fig. 4

Fig. 3

Fig. 6

Fig. 7

Fig. 8

Fig. 9

Fig. 10

Fig. 11

PLATE VI

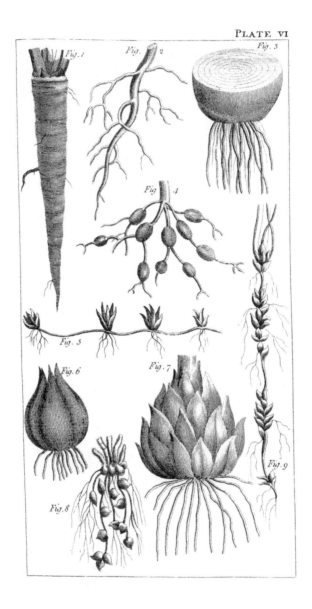

Fig. 1   Fig. 2   Fig. 3

Fig. 4

Fig. 5

Fig. 6   Fig. 7

Fig. 8   Fig. 9

PLATE VII

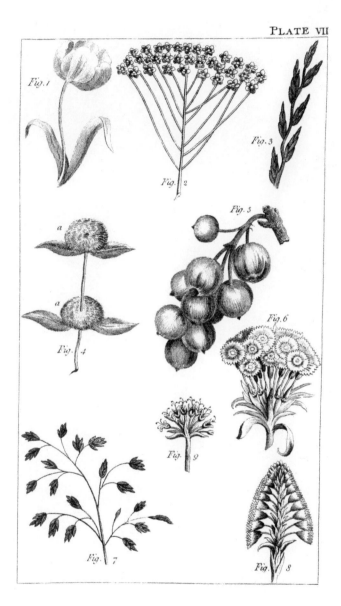

Fig. 1

Fig. 2

Fig. 3

Fig. 5

a

a

Fig. 4

Fig. 6

Fig. 7

Fig. 9

Fig. 8

PLATE VI.

ROOTS.

Fig. 1.   A Spindle-fhaped Root.

Fig. 2.   A Branching or Fibrous Root.

Fig. 3.   A coated Bulbous Root, cut acrofs to fhow the coats that compofe it.

Fig. 4.   A Tuberous Root.

Fig. 5.   A Repent or Creeping Root.

Fig. 6.   A folid Bulb.

Fig. 7.   A fcaly Bulb.

Fig. 8.   A granulous Root.

Fig. 9.   A jointed Root.

———

PLATE VII.

FRUIT-STALKS AND MODES OF FLOWERING.

Fig. 1.   A Stalk that fupports the Flower, and rifes directly from the Root.

Fig. 2.   A Corymbus or broad Spike, as in Gold of Pleafure.

Fig. 3.   A Spike.

Fig. 4.   Verticillus or Whorls, as in Horehound, Mint, &c. ; *a a*, the Whorls.

Fig. 5.   A Racemus or Bunch, as in Currants.

Fig. 6.   A Faficulus or Bundle, as in the Sweet William.

Fig. 7.   A Panicle.

Fig.

Fig. 8.   A Thyrſus, exemplified in the Butter-bur.
Fig. 9.   An Aggregate Flower, ſhown in the Scabioſa.

PLATE VIII. AND IX.

LEAVES.

Fig. 1.   Round.
Fig. 2.   Circular.
Fig. 3.   Egg-ſhaped.
Fig. 4.   Oval.
Fig. 5.   Oblong.
Fig. 6.   Spear-ſhaped.
Fig. 7.   Strap-ſhaped.
Fig. 8.   Awl-ſhaped.
Fig. 9.   Kidney-ſhaped.
Fig. 10.   Heart-ſhaped.
Fig. 11.   Creſcent-ſhaped.
Fig. 12.   Triangular.
Fig. 13.   Arrow-ſhaped.
Fig. 14.   Halbert-ſhaped.
Fig. 15.   Divided or Cleft.
Fig. 16.   Compoſed of three Lobes.
Fig. 17.   Divided to the mid rib.
Fig. 18.   With five Angles.
Fig. 19.   Hand-ſhaped.
Fig. 20.   With winged Clefts.
Fig. 21.   Ditto jagged.
Fig. 22.   Parted.
Fig. 23.   Tooth-like.

Fig.

PLATE.VIII

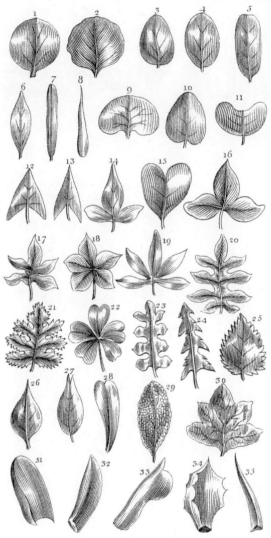

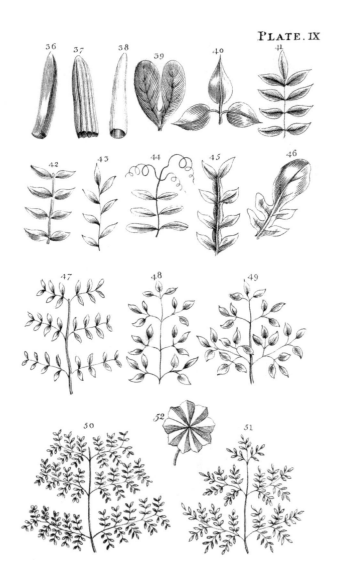

PLATE. IX

Fig. 24. Indentments.

Fig. 25. Serrated or Sawed.

Fig. 26. Ending ſharp or tapering.

Fig. 27. ———— ſharply nicked.

Fig. 28. Wedge.

Fig. 29. Wrinkled.

Fig. 30. Veined.

Fig. 31. Tongue-ſhaped.

Fig. 32. Scimeter-ſhaped.

Fig. 33. Hatched-ſhaped.

Fig. 34. Deltoid, like the old Greek Delta.

Fig. 35. Three-ſided.

Fig. 36. Channelled.

Fig. 37. Furrowed.

Fig. 38. Cylindrical.

Fig. 39. Finger-ſhaped, of two.

Fig. 40. Growing by three on leaf-ſtalks.

Fig. 41. Winged, terminated by an odd one.

Fig. 42. ————, abruptly.

Fig. 43. ————, alternately.

Fig. 44. ————, tendrilled.

Fig. 45. ————, jointedly.

Fig. 46. Lyre-ſhaped.

Fig. 47. Doubly-winged.

Fig. 48. Doubly three-leaved.

Fig. 49. Triply three-leaved.

Fig. 50. Thrice feathered, abruptly terminated.

Fig. 51. Ditto, with an odd one.

Fig. 52. Plaited.

TABLE

PLATE X. AND XI.

DETERMINATE LEAVES, STEMS, SUPPORTS, &c.

Fig. 1.   *a, Inflected,* bent inwards ; when the Leaf is
turned upwards toward the Stem.

    b, Erect, upright ; when the angle they form
with the Stem is very fmall.

    c, Spreading or *Expanding,* patent ; when they
make an acute angle with the Stem.

    d, Horizontal ; when they ftand at right angles
with the Stem.

    e, Reclined, reflex ; when they are bowed
downwards, fo that the Apex or Tip is
lower than the Bafe.

    f, Revolute, rolled back, and downwards.

Fig. 2.   *g, Seminal,* Seed Leaves ; which before were
the Cotyledons, and are the firft which
appear.

    h, Cauline, Stem Leaves, fuch as grow round
the Stem.

    i, Rameous, Branch Leaves.

    k, Floral, Flower Leaves ; fuch as are placed
at the coming out of the Flower.

Fig. 3.   *l, Peltated,* or Shield-fafhioned ; a Leaf which
has the Foot-ftalk inferted into the centre
of the lower difk, or furface, as in the
Water Lily, Jack in a Box, &c.

    m, Petiolated ; when there is a Petiole faftened
to the Leaf at the margin of the bafe.

    n, Decurrent, running down ; when the bafe

of

Plate X.

Fig. 1   Fig. 2   Fig. 3

Fig. 4   Fig. 5   Fig. 6   Fig. 7   Fig. 8

PLATE XI.

Fig. 9

Fig. 10

Fig. 11

Fig. 12

Fig. 13

Fig. 14

Fig. 15

Fig. 16

Fig. 17

of a Seffile Leaf, extends itfelf downwards along the Stem, beyond the proper bafe or termination of the Leaf, as in the Thiftle, Globe Flower.

o, *Seffile*, fquat; when the Leaf has no Petiole, but is faftened immediately to the Stem.

p, *Amplexicaul*, embracing the Stalk; when the bafe of the Leaf embraces the Stem croffways on both fides, or *femiamplexicaul*, half embracing the Stalk, which only differs from the amplexicaul in that it is in a lefs degree.

q, *Perfoliate*, Leaf-pierced; is when the bafe of the Leaf is continued acrofs the Stem, till it meet again, fo as to furround it.

r, *Connate*, growing together; when two oppofite Leaves join, and are united into one, as in Hemp, Agrimony.

f, *Vaginant*, forming a Vagina or Sheath; when the bafe of the Leaf forms a cylindric tube that invefts the branch. This is alfo called a Glove-embracing Leaf, as it goes round the Stem and fhoots from the middle.

Fig. 4.   *t*, *Articulated*, jointed; when one Leaf grows out at the top of the other.

u, *Stellate*, Starry or Verticillate, whorled; when the Stalk is furrounded in Whorls by more than two Leaves: and thefe again receive the denomination of Tern, Quatern, Quina, Sena, &c. according to the number

number of **Leaves** of which the Star or Whorl is compofed, as in African Almond, Rofebay, &c.

w, Quatern, Fourfold. See the laft Definition.

x, Oppofite; when the Cauline Leaves come out in pairs facing each other, and fometimes each pair is croffed by the next, fo that they point four different ways.

y, Alternate; when they come out fingly, and follow in gradual order.

z, Acerofe, Awny, Chaffy; when it is linear and perfifting, as in Pine Tree, and Juniper.

a, Imbricated; when they lie over each other like the tiles of a houfe.

b, Fafciculated, bundled; when many come from the fame point, as in the Larch Tree.

Fig. 5. *Spatulated,* refembling a Spatula; when the figure is roundifh, but lengthened out by the addition of a linear bafe that is narrower.

Fig. 6. *c, Squamofa Culm,* or Straw; when it is covered with imbricate fcales.

d, Repent, creeping; when by lying upon the ground, or touching a tree, wall, &c. they put forth roots at certain intervals, as in Ivy, Trumpet Flower, &c.

Fig. 7. *Frons.* Frond is a fpecies of Trunk, compofed of a Branch and a Leaf blended together, and is frequently united with the fruƈtification; it belongs to Palms, &c.

Fig. 8. *Articulate,* jointed Straw or Culm; when they

they are diftinguifhed from fpace to fpace
by knots or joints.

Fig. 9. *Volubiles*, twining ; when they afcend fpirally, by the branch of fome other plant.
Thefe wind either to the left, according
to the motion of the fun (as it is commonly phrafed) as in Hops, Honeyfuckle, &c.
or to the right, contrary to the fun's motion, as in Bindweed, Malabar Nightfhade,
Kidney Bean, &c.

Fig. 10. *Dichotomous*, forked ; when the divifion is
always in two parts.

Fig. 11. *Brachiatus*, having Arms ; when the branches
are oppofite, and each pair is croffed by
the pair above or below it.

Fig. 12. *e e*, *Bracteæ*, Floral Leaves ; differing in
fhape and colour from the reft, as in the
Lime Tree, Fumitory, &c.

f f, The common Leaves.

Fig. 13. *Pedicled Glands ;* borne on Pedicles, *g g.*

Fig. 14. *Tendril* or Clafper ; *h*, is a filiform fpiral
band, by which a plant faftens itfelf to any
other body, as in the Vine, Heart Pea,
and Trumpet Flower.

i, Concave Glands, are either Petiolar, when
they are on the Petioles, as in the Palma
Chrifti, Paffion Flower, Senfitive Plant, &c.
Foliaceous ; when they are produced from
the Leaves, and thefe are from the Serra-
tures, as in the Willow ; from the Bafe, as
in the Peach, Gourd, &c. from the Back,

as

as in the Tamarisk ; or from the Surface,
as in the Butterwort, Sundew, &c.

Stipular, when they are produced from Stipula, as in Mountain Ebony, &c.

Capillary, like hairs, as in the Currant
Tree, Snap Dragon, &c.

Pores only, as in the Tamarind Tree and
Viscous Campion.

k, Stipula, is a scale or small Leaf, stationed
on each side of the base of the Petioles or
Peduncles when they are first appearing, as
in the Papilionaceous Flowers; also, in
the Tamarind Wild Cherry, Rose, &c.

Fig. 15. *p p*, Opposite Leaves. See Fig. 4.

q q, Axillary, coming out from the Wings ;
that is, either between the Leaf and the
Stem, or between the branch and the Stem.

Fig. 16. *n, Aculeus*, a Prickle, is a kind of Armature,
proceeding from the Cortex of the plant
only, as in the Rose, Bramble, &c.

o, Triple Prickle or Fork.

Fig. 17. *l, Spina*, a Thorn, is a kind of sharp wea-
pon or armature, protruded from the wood
of the plant, as in the Plum Tree, Buckthorn, &c. It will often disappear by
culture, as in the Pear.

m, A Triple Spine.

F I N I S.